Panentheism and Cosmopolitanism

Benedikt Paul Göcke

Panentheism and Cosmopolitanism

A Very Short Introduction to the Philosophy of Karl Christian Friedrich Krause (1781-1832)

PETER LANG

Berlin · Bruxelles · Chennai · Lausanne · New York · Oxford

Library of Congress Cataloging-in-Publication Data
A CIP catalog record for this book has been applied for at the
Library of Congress.

Bibliographic information published by the Deutsche
Nationalbibliothek. The German National Library lists this publication
in the German National Bibliography; detailed bibliographic
data is available on the Internet at http://dnb.d-nb.de.

ISBN 978-3-631-89624-2 (Print)
E-ISBN 978-3-631-91376-5 (E-PDF)
E-ISBN 978-3-631-91377-2 (EPUB)
DOI 10.3726/ b21700

© 2024 Benedikt Paul Göcke
Published by Peter Lang GmbH, Berlin, Deutschland

info@peterlang.com - www.peterlang.com

Open Access: This work is licensed under a Creative Commons Attribution
CC-BY 4.0 license. To view a copy of this license, visit
https://creativecommons.org/ licenses/by/4.0/
This publication has been peer reviewed.

All the commandments according to which each individual human being should form his life are contained in one thing: Be human! Or: be God-like within the limits of your essence, your humanity!

(Krause 1843: 513)

Humanity is undoubtedly destined to unfold its life as one organic and all-harmonious whole.

(Krause 1811a: 1)

Contents

Preface 9

Introduction 11
1. A Glimpse at the Life of Karl Christian Friedrich Krause .. 17
2. Krause and the Vedic Traditions 21
   2.1 The Vedic Traditions as the Origin of Science and Art 21
   2.2 The Four Principles of Philosophy 25
   2.3 Panentheism and the Vedic Traditions 27
3. Krause's Panentheism 31
   3.1 The Analytical and the Synthetic Part of Philosophy 32
   3.2 The Thought of the Absolute 34
      3.2.1 The Ego as a Self-Same and Whole Being 35
      3.2.2 The Ego as Body and Spirit 36
      3.2.3 The Ego is not the Absolute 37
      3.2.4 The Concept of the World and the Absolute as the Ultimate Ground of the World 39
      3.2.5 The Infinite and Unconditioned Absolute 40
   3.3 The Vision of the Absolute 41
   3.4 The Absolute and the Principle of Sufficient Reason 44
   3.5 The Absolute as the One, Whole and Independent Being 45
   3.6 Panentheism, Mereology and the Priority of the Whole 48
4. Krause's Cosmopolitanism 53
   4.1 Social Theory, Cosmopolitanism, and the Concept of the Human League 54
      4.1.1 The Human League 55
      4.1.2 The Equal Value of All Human Beings 57
      4.1.3 The Human League and Cosmopolitism 58
   4.2 The Structure of the Human League 60
      4.2.1 The Fundamental Societies: Marriage, Friendship, and Free Socializing 61

  4.2.2 The Laboring Societies for the Fundamental Forms of Life 65
  4.2.3 The Laboring Societies for the Fundamental Works of Life 70
 4.3 The Many Dimensions of Freedom 71
  4.3.1 Freedom as the Driving Force of the Human League 72
  4.3.2 Freedom as the Goal of the Human League 73
  4.3.3 Cosmopolitanism and Cultural Diversity 74
 4.4 Utopia of the Not-Yet 76

Conclusion 79

Bibliography 81

Preface

This short book is based on several of my works on Karl Christian Friedrich Krause's philosophy. Bits and pieces to be found here have been published previously in the following places: (1) *The Panentheism of Karl Christian Friedrich Krause (1781–1832). From Transcendental Philosophy to Metaphysics.* Oxford, Berlin: Peter Lang. 2018. (2) *Alles in Gott? Zur Aktualität des Panentheismus Karl Christian Friedrich Krauses.* Friedrich Pustet. 2012. (3) (with Claus Dierksmeier): *The Philosophy and Theology of Karl Christian Friedrich Krause.* In: European Journal for Philosophy of Religion. Vol 14 (2). 2022. (4) "Panentheism as Cosmopolitanism. Karl Christian Friedrich Krause's Conception of the Human League." In: *Religious Studies*. Online First. 2023. 1–16. (5) "On the Importance of Karl Christian Friedrich Krause's Panentheism." In: *Zygon. Journal of Religion and Science*. Vol. 48 (2). 2013. 364–379. (6) "Gott und die Welt? Bemerkungen zu Karl Christian Friedrich Krauses System der Philosophie." In: *Theologie und Philosophie*. Vol. 87. 2012. 25–45. (7) "Das Urbild der Menschheit. Panentheismus als kosmopolitische Gesellschaftstheorie." In: Benedikt Paul Göcke, Johannes Seidel SJ (Hrsg.): *Karl Christian Friedrich Krause: Das Urbild der Menschheit*. Philosophische Bibliothek. Hamburg: Meiner-Verlag. 2022. ix–cvii. (8) "Essential Features of Karl Christian Friedrich Krause's Idealistic Panentheism." In: Benedikt Paul Göcke, Joshua Farris (Eds.): *Handbook on Idealism and Immaterialism*. London: Routledge. 2021. 260–276. (9) "Indian in Nature? Karl Christian Friedrich Krause's Panentheism and the Vedic Traditions." In: Benedikt Paul Göcke, Swami Medhananda (Eds.): *Panentheism in Indian and Western Thought. Cosmopolitan Interventions*. London: Routledge. 2023.

Introduction

Karl Christian Friedrich Krause (1781–1832) left for posterity an impressive and astonishingly contemporary corpus of philosophical creativity.[1] Not only does it cover numerous topics of theoretical and practical philosophy, from a panentheistic-cosmopolitan point of view[2], but, in terms of the history of philosophy, it may be seen as one of the first works from a European pen which appreciates the Indian roots of European thinking in their systematic importance. As Krause states:

> I thought, as early as 1807, that the reunification of the European peoples with the Indians and with Indian science and art, will bring about a more important change [...] than the so-called restoration of science after the conquest of Constantinople by the Turks. (Krause 1891: 270)[3]

The list of Krause's writings comprises 256 works, plus the handwritten *Nachlass*, which is a good twenty meters long, kept in the Saxon State Library in Dresden.[4] All the works published in Krause's lifetime, the unpublished writings, and his handwritten *Nachlass*, await historical-critical examination, a complete edition, and a wider reception and appreciation in German and Anglo-Saxon philosophy.

German and Anglo-Saxon philosophy turned away from Krause, after a brief heyday of German Krausism in the nineteenth century, which featured Hermann von Leonhardi, Heinrich Simon Lindemann, Heinrich Ahrens, Carl Röder, August Wünsche and Paul Hohlfeld.[5] This ignorance of Krause is surprising because Krausism was definitely effective and was acting at the forefront of modernity: The Krausists were not only closely connected to the General German Women's Association (*Allgemeiner Deutscher Frauenverein*) and the Fröbelian General Educational

---

1 All translations from German sources into English are due to Stephen Priest (Oxford University) or myself. Reference is to the German original.
2 See also Wollgast (1990: 65): "Krause has taken an independent position in almost all areas of philosophy. This includes: philosophy of language, jurisprudence, ethics, aesthetics, philosophy of religion, and philosophy of science, especially mathematics."
3 Cf. also Krause (1890a: 184): "It was only in 1815 that I started to read mystical writings. Previously, I had only read parts of Jacob Böhme, in 1799, part of German theology in 1812, and part of Oupnekhat in 1807. It is remarkable how many images, discourses, and propositions which I found presented, I find again in the mystics, and for the most part clearer and better, e.g. in Oupnekhat."
4 See the extensive list of publications in Ureña/Fuchs (2007: xxxvii–lxxii).
5 For an analysis of German Krausism, see Ureña (2007) and Ureña (2001).

Association (Fröbelianischer *Allgemeiner Erziehungsverein*) led by Bertha von Marenholtz-Bülow, and there campaigned for equal rights for women and the rights of children—both unions "considered Krause to be the first philosopher who philosophically justified the equal rights of women" (Ureña 2007: 312–312)—but the Krausists also organized international philosophers' congresses in Prague in 1868, and in Frankfurt am Main in 1869, at which women were not only present but also actually had their say.

The reason often given for the turn away from the study of Krause is that his philosophy became incomprehensible and obscurantist, due to the many neologisms that he had introduced. The difficulty in getting used to Krause's *Wesensprache* ('*language of Essence*'), however, is no good reason to ignore Krause's philosophy, because, from a logical point of view, it is quite precise and expressive, and, more importantly, it is also increasingly found only in Krause's private notes and late publications. The vast majority of his published works are written in pleasant prose. Furthermore, Krause himself was aware that his neologistic 'language of Essence' (*Wesensprache*), as well as his pasigraphy, would meet with resistance:

> My scientific expressions may strike those who are used to the prevailing usage of language, and those who do not suspect the importance of a short, appropriate designation of the basic truths of Science and life, let alone understand, as tasteless and pedantic, and to be laughed at and ridiculed. But they are, nevertheless, understood by connoisseurs. And, because they are intrinsically beautiful, and at the same time appropriate to the art of education and teaching, are also accepted. (Krause 1890: 80)[6]

The minimal involvement of German and Anglo-Saxon philosophy with Krause is all the more surprising when one considers that Krause is recognized in Spain and Latin America as one of the greatest German philosophers. The reason for this esteem is that Krause's philosophy has been a major driving force of Spanish and Latin American modernity and enormously influenced, if not subcutaneously enabled, Latin American liberation philosophy and theology. As Wollgast (1990: 71) pointedly puts

---

6 Frege's *Begriffsschrift*, which pursued the same goal, was more fortunate. On Krause's indirect influence on Frege, via C. Fortlage, who campaigned for Frege's professorship in Jena, and also, on Krause's indirect influence thereby on current analytical philosophy, see Kreiser (2001: 155). Meixner (2022) not only argues that Krause's logic is very close to Frege's system in its expressive power, but also that Venn diagrams should actually be called "Krause Diagrams," because Krause was the first to develop a completely combinatorial representation of syllogistics.

it: "No German philosopher has influenced the intellectual development of Spain and large parts of Latin America as much as Krause." And Krumpel (1990: 166) argues that "the best traditions of German humanistic thought are reflected in Krause's philosophy: a way of thinking that was extremely effective in Spain and Latin America, and made a significant contribution to international understanding."

Krause's influence in Spain and Latin America was essentially promoted by Julián Sanz del Río, who was sent from Spain to Germany in 1843, for a two-year study, to find out about the philosophical debates that were going on at the time, so that, on his return, he might strengthen Spanish discussions by introducing the discourses conducted in Central Europe. As Wirmer-Donos (2001: 78) states:

> The trip to Germany which the Spanish canon lawyer and Professor of the History of Philosophy Julián Sanz del Río (1814–1869) undertook in 1843, is of fundamental importance for the development of Krausism, as a political and spiritual movement. By decree of the Spanish Liberal Minister of Education, Gomez de la Serna, Sanz del Río was appointed Professor of Jurisprudence at the University of Madrid from June 16, 1843, and obliged to study in Germany for two years.

On his journey, Sanz del Río came into contact with the first generation of Krause students around Hermann von Leonhardi and Heinrich Ahrens, and was so impressed by Krause's system of philosophy that back in Spain he published a work entitled *Ideal de la Humanidad para la Vida* (1860), which purportedly reproduces, in del Río's own words, some of the central ideas of Krause's philosophy that could be found in Krause's 1811 *Das Urbild der Menschheit* (*The Human Archetype*).

This book, the *Ideal de la Humanidad para la Vida*, hit the core of the prevailing cultural and philosophical need for a consistent rationalism, and became the founding document of Spanish Krausismo, which was one of the dominant cultural forces in Spain up to the time of Franco, and has left traces even in the Argentine Constitution.[7] Interestingly enough, through the pontificate of pope Francis, Krausism also gained influence, at least subcutaneously, in the Roman Catholic Church. As Dierksmeier (2016: 5) puts it, after an analysis of the papal encyclical *Laudato si*:

---

7 · See Landau (1995: 5–6): "Krausismo has also found many followers in Portugal, and many Latin American countries, as far away as Argentina. In Europe, the influence of Krause's thinking may also be found outside of the Iberian Peninsula, in Italy, Belgium, the Netherlands and Scotland. In France, Proudhon was influenced by him." Cf., on the history of Krausismo, also Dierksmeier (2008), Rubio (2017), Krumpel (2001), the contributions in Ferreia (2021), López-Morillas (1981), Mateo (1982), Dierksmeier (2013), Jiménez García (1994), and Schmitz (2000).

> If one compares Krause's philosophy with the writings of the Pope, one immediately notices a great deal of agreement between the two thinkers. This emerges particularly clearly in their respective cosmopolitan orientation towards the goal of the pacification of natural and social living conditions, to be brought about through responsible individual and institutional freedom.[8]

However, as Ureña (1988) has been able to prove, Sanz del Río's *Ideal de la Humanidad para la Vida* is by no means a Spanish *adaptation* of Krause's ideas, but is a *literal* translation of a shorter work by Krause called *Entfaltung und urbildliche Darstellung der Idee des Menschheitbundes, vom Standorte des Lebens aus* (*Development and Archetypical Presentation of the Idea of the Human League, from the Standpoint of Life*), which Krause published in 1811 in his newspaper *Tagblatt des Menschheitlebens (Daily Paper of the Life of Humanity)* (Krause 1811a). As a matter of fact, Spanish *Krausismo* is therefore immediately rooted in Krause's work. As Ureña (1991: 14) states:

> The book *Ideal de la Humanidad para la Vida* (1860) by Julián Sanz del Río, which has been described as "the book of hours" of the *Hispanicized* "Krauismo", is a *verbatim* translation of two essays, which Krause had published in 1811. Sanz del Río concealed this origin, and presented the mentioned writing as an independent accommodation of basic Krausist ideas to Spanish conditions. This discovery undermines the widespread thesis of a "Krauismo" largely independent of Krause's work, and remodeled in the spirit of Spain.

Therefore, although German Krausism lost importance toward the end of the nineteenth century, and Krause fell into oblivion in his home country, one may again agree with Wollgast (1990: 65) when he put it succinctly:

> Next to 19th Century Germany, the world of Krause's influence [...] is Spain, which encompasses about 4/5 of the Pyrenees Peninsula, and the continent of South America with about 17.8 million km^2.

Against this background, it would therefore be desirable for German and Anglo-Saxon philosophy to turn toward one of those thinkers who, viewed globally, must be regarded as one of the most influential German philosophers of all. The purpose of this very short introduction is to foster a better understanding of Krause's philosophy and, hopefully, to arouse lasting interest to deal with Krause's system of philosophy in depth. To achieve this purpose, Chapter 1 briefly states some highlights of Krause's

---

[8] For a careful, and partly speculative, study of Krause's influence on the Cuban Revolution, see Gott (2002).

life before Chapter 2 turns to the Vedic roots of Krause's panentheism, which then is elaborated in some detail in Chapter 3. Chapter 4 spells out Krause's cosmopolitanism, which is firmly based on, and a consequence, of his panentheism.

1. A Glimpse at the Life of Karl Christian Friedrich Krause

Krause was born on May 6, 1781 in Eisenberg, a small town in Thuringia. He spent the early years of schooling in Eisenberg, before joining the Convent School in Donndorf, in Easter 1792. In 1794 Krause returned to the Eisenberg Lyceum. He remained there until his father took a new job, as pastor in Nobitz, in 1795. On July 11, 1797, Krause passed the leaving examination at the gymnasium in the nearby town of Altenburg, and enrolled in the same year at the University of Jena, which had a major, albeit tragic, role to play in his future.

In Jena, Krause "heard lectures by the theologians Griesbach, Paul, Ilgen and Jacobi; the philosophers Fichte, Schütz, Eichstädt, Schelling, and A. W. Schlegel; and the scientists Voigt, Succow, Loder, Bretschneider, Batsch, Lenz, Graumüller, Göttling and Stahl" (Ureña 1991: 30). Although it had been the father's wish that Krause primarily devote himself to the study of theology in Jena, Krause decided, without completely dismissing his father's suggestion, to follow his own interests, and began a profound study of mathematics and philosophy.

Krause was awarded the degree of Doctor of Philosophy on October 6, 1801, with a thesis on the "Forbidding of the White Lie" and a work entitled *Disquisitio mathematica de inventione numerorum primorum et factorum compositorum* ('Mathematical discourse on the first discovery of numbers and the combining of factors'). Shortly after, he passed the theological candidates examination.

During the time of his *Habilitation*, at the beginning of his career as a young lecturer (*Privatdozent*) Krause fell in love with Amalie Concordia Fuchs. Amalie was the daughter of a wine merchant from Eisenberg. Although his father spoke out against this relationship due to various rumors concerning the integrity of Amalie, Karl and Amalie decided to marry publicly, on July 19, 1802. In a marriage that lasted 30 years, Karl and Amalie had 14 children, 12 of whom would survive their parents.

In 1802, Krause passed his *Habilitation*, in Jena, with the work *de philosophiae et matheseos notione et earum intima coniunctione* ('Concerning philosophical and mathematical notions and their intimate conjunction'). The public disputation was held on April 2, 1802. Afterward, he offered lectures in logic, natural law, and pure mathematics, for the summer semester. Despite the fact that these lectures had not been announced in advance, he found an audience for all of them. In 1803, Krause lectured on logic and metaphysics, natural philosophy, natural law, and pure mathematics. In the winter semester of 1803/1804, Krause lectured on the *System der Natur- und Transcendentalphilosophie nach Diktaten* ('System of Natural and Transcendental Philosophy') and *Reine Mathematik n.s. Compendium* ('Pure Mathematics'). A year later, he announced his last lectures in Jena. But he left the city two weeks before the lectures were due to start, and settled briefly in the small town of Rudolstadt. Despite the pleas of his students, his patrons, and his father, Krause could not be persuaded to continue his work as a lecturer at the University of Jena because he did no longer expect to obtain a permanent position there.

Although there was no prospect of any permanent position in Rudolstadt, Krause remained there from the beginning of October 1804 to April 1805. He looked back on his time in the small village with affection: "I gained a lot by pulling out to Rudolstadt, to be sure, not immediately in money, but in insight and peace of mind; in Jena I should have acquired nothing of money anyway, and little of the higher possessions either" (Krause 1903: 108).

On April 6, 1805, Krause moved to Dresden, with his family. He traveled via Altenburg, and was recorded on 5 April in the Masonic Lodge "Archimedes at the Three Drawing Boards." On October 31, he became affiliated to the Dresden Lodge "The Three Swords and the True Friends." Krause committed to the Freemasons because of the ideal of human coexistence he saw formulated in Masonic writings. It had now to be shown that this could be extended to the whole of society, with the aim of its transformation into an integrated league of humanity. This hope, which grounded Krause's lifelong high regard for the Masons, was bitterly disappointed in reality and led, after a rapid rise in his career in the lodge, to his expulsion on 17 December 1810. The ground for this was the imminent publication of his work 'The Three Oldest Art Documents of the Masonic Brotherhood' (*Die drei ältesten Kunsturkunden der Freimaurerbrüderschaft*). In this particular publication, Krause took the side of the reformist Freemasons, against the traditionalists who wanted to ensure Masonic writings were published and controlled only within the lodges, especially those which concerned Masonic liturgy.

Apart from the dispute with the Masons, Krause's first stay in Dresden is characterized by the fact that he still needed to keep himself afloat through giving private lessons, and needed the continued financial support of his father. In addition to the education of his children, to which he devoted several hours a day, he worked on writings on Freemasonry, sculpture, architecture, painting, music, the natural sciences, mathematics, geography, politics, society, ethics, natural law and linguistics (cf. Ureña 1991: 269). Although these topics are today classified as independent areas of science, it was clear to Krause that together they make up a single organic system of science:

> That I am dealing with all sorts of things, I do at the urging of my spirit; it is nothing without unity, and there is nothing here that is not necessary to my main work, the system. I have still not exhausted this wealth of knowledge, and I cannot do anything else. (Krause 1903: 190)

Krause's residence in Dresden was not of long duration. After just a few years, he and his family moved to the small Saxon town of Tharandt because of the advancing army of Napoleon. He remained there for several months before moving with his family to an apartment in Berlin's Friedrichstrasse, on November 24, 1813. On arrival, Krause tried for a job at the University of Berlin. However, after some seeming initial success, he suffered a similar fate as in Jena: Because, in Krause's view, the student numbers were too low to justify courses, he decided

> to announce no courses for the next six months; because when I do announce them and cannot keep up, I regret making my announcement. And I would not be able keep them up, because I cannot live if I do not receive 200 thalers for such a lecture, for which I would need an audience of 40. And I cannot count on that, because there are still barely 100 students here [at the University]. (Krause 1903: 332)

As in Jena, Krause was not persuaded by the advice of his friends to offer his lectures independently, on the hope of eventually receiving a secure position. It is therefore no surprise that Krause did not get the Chair of Philosophy freed up by Fichte's death.

Because this chance of obtaining a permanent position came to nothing, Krause decided to give up the profession of private tutor completely, in order to develop his System of Science. Together with his family, he moved back to Dresden on May 10, 1815. Krause settled at the Große Meißnische Gasse (cf. Wollgast 2016: 25). This house was not only within walking distance of the *Japanischer Palais*, in which the Royal Library with its collection of Indian and Asiatic Philosophy was accommodated, and was where the Masonic lodge *Asträa* held their meetings, but, most interestingly, it was also the home of Arthur Schopenhauer, who had been living there since April 1814. Krause and Schopenhauer's shared time in the Große Meißnische Gasse ended when Schopenhauer traveled to Italy on September 24, 1818, and was only interrupted once, by Krause's journey to Italy from Easter 1817 to January 1818. When Schopenhauer returned from Italy in 1819, he did not come back to the flat in the Große Meißnische Gasse, and started to live exclusively in the Ostra-Allee 897 until he left Dresden in 1819 to pick up his new position in Berlin. Meanwhile Krause also decided to move into a more affordable flat in a house in the Reitbahngasse in Dresden, where he stayed until he moved to Göttingen in 1823 to make another fresh start. However, due to the death of his 78-year-old father in 1825, who still financially supported Krause and his family, Krause was forced to deliver as many lectures as possible in Göttingen, making him turn away from working on his own philosophical writings. Rather as in Berlin, a Chair, this time left vacant by the death of Friedrich Ludwig Bouterwecks, was snatched away from in front of him, on this occasion by Amadeus Wendt of Leipzig. It is understandable that, during the time in Göttingen, Krause often looked back with nostalgia at the beginning of his career in Jena:

> If I had not withdrawn from university teaching in the year 1804, or had even just remained vigorous and up to date as a writer, I would now be in a position of outstanding effectiveness, which a Fries or a Hegel [...] would certainly not overlook. (Krause 1900: 330)

Krause's difficult financial and professional situation was exacerbated by an extremely awkward political mishap, when he was suspected of having been involved in the Göttingen student and civil rebellion of January 8–16, 1831 because, at that time, he received large sums of money which, one of his opponents claimed, came from the Paris Revolutionary Committee: "In fact, this was part of an inheritance" (Wollgast: 1990: 13).

To spare Krause being prosecuted by the police and the legal authorities, and because Krause had long planned to leave Göttingen in order to move to Munich, he was given an ultimatum to do so immediately. Krause obeyed, but was weakened by the charges against him, and dejected. He also had just as little prospect of a secure existence in Munich as in Göttingen. Krause now stood without bread or wages, and had to begin to sell his books, and pawn other property. In the last shock of his life, he was forced by a police decree to leave Munich on 17 March 1832. He was accused of acting with depravity toward the students who were affiliated to him (cf. Ureña 1991: 622). King Ludwig ultimately rescinded the expulsion order after the intervention of sympathetic government ministers like Franz von Baader, but Krause was nonetheless forbidden from teaching at the University. Schelling seems to have been responsible. His reason was that "Munich University as a whole was closed. One was not permitted to take in any new elements" (Ureña 1991: 620).

On September 27, 1832, Karl Christian Friedrich Krause died impoverished, lonely and without, in his own lifetime, being able to bring about the good he had hoped: to lead humanity to a better future through the study of philosophy.

2. Krause and the Vedic Traditions

Krause was one of the first European philosophers—unlike Hegel—to appreciate, and draw upon, Indian philosophical and theological traditions. Moreover, his panentheistic system of philosophy can be seen as a modern version of ancient Indian philosophical thought. In what follows, Krause's appreciation of the Indian traditions is spelled out in more detail before central features of his panentheism are clarified from a systematic point of view. The latter of which will be considered in the next chapter.

2.1 The Vedic Traditions as the Origin of Science and Art

Geographically, Krause defined India as follows:

> India comprises the oldest peoples on the Sind, Gang (Ganges) and Buramputer-rivers, on the entire southern slopes of the high mountains of Asia, over peninsulas on both sides as far as Selan (or Zeilon) and the peninsula of Malaka. (Krause 1885: 64–65)

This part of the world, according to Krause, was the historical birthplace of human education and civilization[9]:

> Even if the whole of humanity of the ancient earth did not emanate from India, rather from High Asia, nevertheless human education—civilization did. (Krause 1887: 34)
>
> From India, along with the entire social education, with science and art, music also seems to have spread across Asia, Upper Africa and Europe. (Krause 1827: 74)

According to Krause, the Vedas, the Upaniṣads, the *Mahābhārata* (which includes the *Bhagavad Gītā*), and the *Rāmāyaṇa*, for the first time in human history, presented numerous metaphysical truths about empirical reality, its ultimate foundation, the goal of life and the ways to achieve it.[10] In terms of their wisdom, the Vedas, according to Krause, who had a strict Lutheran education, even outrank the Bible, and should be considered as "the root and the trunk" (Krause 1891: 52) of the religious life of humanity:

---

9   Krause (1843a: 254) criticizes Schleiermacher for his ignorance of the Indian traditions and for his argument that the history of monotheism starts with the Abrahamitic religions.

10 Cf. Krause (1885: 65–66): "But even more instructive are the oldest epic poems of the Indians: Mahabharata and Ramajana […] Several fragments of these individual poems have already been made known, and they are without doubt up to now the greatest epic poems of this earth, richest in content."

> All the essentials that are contained in the Bible, for example, can also be recognized by pure reason, and much more purely and better and more deeply and unfolded and shaped, and have been recognized better long ago, indeed long before Moses lived (see the Veds and the Vedanta philosophy), as has been proven by history. (Krause 1892: 73)

Sanskrit, therefore, is not only one of the most important languages in the world, but, in fact, "the mother of our original language" (Krause 1903: 45) of which Persian, Greek, Latin, and German are derived, the latter of which, according to Krause, has a special relation to Sanskrit:

> In the first place, I cannot concede to any language on earth the rank before the German language than to the Sangscrida language. The perusal of all the writings of Fr. Bartolomaeo (especially Vyàcarana), even more than the study of Wilkin's Grammar of the Sangscrida language, London, 1808, has taught me that this ancient language deserves the prize [...] and that the German language owes by far the greatest number of its roots and root-words, as well as its endings (inflections) and wordlings (prefixes, indefinites and endings) to the Sangscrida as its mother tongue, and that therefore German linguistics can be enlightened especially by the knowledge of the Sangscrida. [...] Therefore, at the same time, we see in the Sangscrida language in part a historical model, according to which our vernacular language can be refined, purified and further developed in accordance with its own historical mother tongue. (Krause 1816: 14–15)[11]

Krause not only recommended learning Sanskrit as an essential language for philosophical reflection[12] but also felt the need to publish his own system of philosophy in Sanskrit: "It is also a duty to present the system of science, at least the analytical part, in Sanskrit, Greek and Latin as soon as possible" (Krause 1907: 39). Krause, in fact, could have done this as he seemed to have mastered Sanskrit to a sufficient degree:

> Precise knowledge (*Genaue Kenntnis*) of the Brahmanic Sanskrit language has convinced me that this language, especially as it appears in its strict old form in the Vedams, is an original language formed with a scientific spirit. (Krause 1820: 107 FN)

Against this background, it is no surprise that, according to Krause, the European rediscovery of the Indian traditions in the early nineteenth century is of ultimate concern for the future development of philosophy, the

---

11 Cf. also Proksch (1880: 65), and Krause (1885: 28): "[T]he Persian, Greek, Latin and German languages, on the other hand, are closely related sister languages, or daughter languages of Sanskrit."
12 Krause (1891: 279): "For those who can go further, Sanskrit is also recommended, and in fact, from the point of view of linguistic history, as the first essential language."

arts, and the sciences—even more so than the changes from the Western Middle Ages to Western Modernity:

> That the reunification of the European peoples with the Indians and with Indian science and art would bring about a more important change [...] than the so-called restoration of the sciences after the conquest of Constantinople by the Turks, I already thought in 1807 and realised even more clearly in 1814 and 1815, when I gained even more detailed knowledge of the Indian books. (Krause 1891: 270)[13]

Krause was aware that the Vedas, like the Holy Scriptures of the Christian religion, were written by many authors and collected over a long period of time:

> The pieces that make up the Veds are from different times and by different authors (as well as the Old Testament). (Krause 1886: 37)

Krause also knew that Vjassa classified the Vedas into four parts:

> a) Djedir or Jad-jur-ved, which contains all the prose, b) Rig- or Rak-Ved, which contains all the poetry, c) Sam-ved, which contains all the liturgical hymns, d) Atharva- or Atharban-Ved, which contains all the sayings. From these four books, in about the 6th century B.C., a literally faithful excerpt was made, containing all the scientific, dogmatic, i.e. the whole teaching of the Ved, with the omission of all that is merely liturgical, in 50 Oupnek'hats or Upanishads (i.e. secreta tegenda). (Krause 1887: 35)

Furthermore, Krause was also aware that different philosophical systems emerged in India, comparable both to the variety of philosophical systems developed in ancient Greece and to the different schools of theological thinking to be found in Christian Scholasticism. As Krause says:

> For thousands of years a large number of philosophical systems have developed in India itself, which, without the Greeks having had knowledge of the Indians or

---

13 Cf. also Riedel (1954: 234): "That the intimate contact of the European peoples with Indian science and art would usher in a more important change in Western morals than the so-called Renaissance on the threshold from the Middle Ages to modern times; Schopenhauer first heard this prediction from Karl Chr. Fr. Krause, to whom this vision had already dawned a decade ago." The difference between the interpretations of the Indian traditions in Krause and Schopenhauer consists in a difference of the interpretation of ultimate reality: "Karl Krause endeavoured to link his theory of nature to the primordial wisdom of India, Schopenhauer thought in the spirit of Buddha. For the latter, nature was sheer Maya, for the former, the body of God." Cf. also Göcke (2020) for a further analysis of Schopenhauer and Krause. For an analysis of Hegel's India, see Rathore/Mohapatra (2018).

the Indians having had knowledge of the Greeks, form a similar structure to the systems of Greek philosophy. (Krause 1887: 40)

Based on the literature on the Indian traditions available to him, Krause distinguished five orthodox and three non-orthodox systems of Indian philosophy: Vedānta, Nyāya, Sāṃkhya, Mīmāṃsā, and Pātañjala Yoga, according to Krause, constitute the orthodox traditions based on the Vedas, while Jainas, Bauddhas, and Cārvākas deny the authority of the Vedas (cf. Krause 1887: 41–43).

According to Krause (1887: 41 fn), the Vedānta-System is close to Platonism, probably because on Platonism, like on Krause's understanding of Vedanta, the empirical world is not really real. Krause thus explicitly rejected the *Vedanta-System* because on *his* understanding of Vedānta, Vedanta is synonymous with Advaita Vedānta and entails the false doctrine of Māyā. As Krause says:

> The main tenet of this system is that the One Indivisible Being, as such, has no particular qualities, and therefore can be said to be Nothing (*das Nichts*)—that is, nothing finite (*nichts Endliches*). When God is at rest, there is no world of physical matter (*Leibwelt*) or of living beings (*Geistwelt*). But when God is subject to the drive of infinite longing (*Triebe des unendlichen Sehnens*), the world comes forth as the infinite dream of the divine imagination, of Maya. God, as Maya, creates the world in which God reveals Himself to Himself. Nothing in the world has an independent existence. (Krause 1887: 41)

On Krause's view, the biggest mistake of this philosophical system, however, is the very doctrine of Maya:

> A basic error of primal Indian philosophy is that the world of the senses with all its forms is only a deception, only a fantasy play of Brahma with himself—Maja. (Krause 1892: 271)

The reason the doctrine of Maya has to be rejected, according to Krause, consists in the fact that empirical reality ultimately exists and should rather be understood as a divine poem in which humanity plays a significant and substantial role:

> The doctrine of Maya is a misunderstanding of the idea that the world is an essential poem of God, as the original artist. In order to understand this idea, the reality of the human world must be recognized. (Krause 1892: 271)[14]

Apart from this critique of Advaita Vedānta, Krause did not have a great exegetical interest in the question which of the Indian systems is

---

14 Cf. Medhananda (2022) for a critique and analysis of Krause's understanding of Vedanta, cf. also Glasenapp (1956) for a short analysis of Krause's stance on Indian philosophy.

philosophically most faithful to the spirit of the Vedas. Instead, he proposed his own interpretation of what he took to be the main insights of the Vedas, which

> show themselves, as far as our historical knowledge reaches, to be the first independent and peculiar whole of the formation of science, which in regard to the intuition of the Absolute, and concerning the organism of all knowledge formed therein, were essentially completed on earth and in this respect cannot be surpassed or extended. (Krause 1887: 472)

2.2 The Four Principles of Philosophy

Krause's interpretation of the Vedic traditions is based on what he identified as the four underlying philosophical axioms shaping the Vedas' principal philosophical outlook on reality, which Krause, as we shall see, wholeheartedly endorsed:

(1) *The Primacy of Knowledge*: Knowledge is a necessary condition for personal salvation and the prevention of evil:

> The Indians recognise knowledge as the first foundation of all good, but ignorance as the first cause of all evil; they realise that without knowledge the spirit cannot attain to true freedom, to pure selfhood,—to the highest good. (Krause 1887: 44)

(2) *The Primacy of God*: God, that is, the ultimate foundation and ground of empirical reality, is the proper and, ultimately, the only object of knowledge:

> What is particularly remarkable, however, is the basic feature of ancient Indian education: that science [*Wissenschaft*] prevails in its entire life, and specifically pure science, the highest part of philosophical knowledge, which we commonly call metaphysics. [...] According to the Indian system of science [*Wissenschaft*], science is the knowledge of God. (Krause 1885: 66)

(3) *The Primacy of Existential Transformation*: There is a close connection between knowledge, spirituality, and the transformation of one's own existence, because to gain knowledge of ultimate reality is a kind of prayer and meditation. Knowledge of ultimate reality and religious devotion do not exclude, but condition and enhance, each other:

> Yes, it may be said, if it is correctly understood, that scientific research and scientific observation is a prayer of the spirit, which is in itself contained in the call: Essence! God! [Krause could have easily added "Om" here, BPG.][15] It is evident from this that the finite spirit researching science [*Wissenschaft*]

---

15 See Krause (1834: 376): "Essence [is] [...] called Om in the Indian language."

knows itself before God, in God, and always has God's infinite personality before its eyes; it is therefore absolutely certain that scientific research is a godly, religious act; called by ordinary names, a worship of God in spirit and in truth. [...] From this emerges the pure, profound, even genuinely scientific, intrinsic, religious sense of the fact that the Indian scientific researchers, philosophers and mathematicians begin all their scientific works with unification, with a prayer. (The scientific reason for this is correctly stated in the Oupnek'hat T. II. p. 399.) (Krause 1828: 385–386 FN)[16]

(4) *The Proper Goal of Life*: The goal of life is to become similar to God. Krause makes this point while explaining the metaphysics of the word "Om" (Krause 1821: 464):

> The Ved's teach to pronounce the word OM with thought, with contemplation and mind, and declare it to be profound and beautiful according to its individual sounds; this pronouncement is thus recommended by them as a part of becoming similar to God, which contributes to being constantly before God in spirit and mind, and to keeping oneself present before God in God, for, as the Ved's teach: "He who knows God becomes God," [...] that is, such a one becomes similar to God, although in the finite. (Oupn. I p. 393 f.).

> Insofar as the word "Essence" means "God", whether spoken singularly or in context, it is not only to be emphasized more strongly, but also to be pronounced with a sense of meaning that comes to the essence of its

---

16 In support of this interpretation, Krause refers to the translation of the Prashna-Upanishad in Duperron's Oupnek'hat, Vol. 2: 397–399: "Et Oum, quod ab omni magnitudinem habet (majus est), hoc est, quod, quoad (si) in principio quorumlibet quatuor (librorum) Beid, hoc non legat, vires τῶν *Beidha* minus fiat; et cum (legenti) seipsos mercedem non largitur. [...] Athrba, quemadmodum modus τε ostad (praeceptoris) et discipulorum est, (eum modum) cum loco ut attulit, cum illis dixit: nomen magnum, quod in principio [mei] Beid est, quod Athrban Beid sit, illud discipuli mei in principio τῶν *Beidha*, in principio cujusvis âjet τῶν *Beidha*, pronunciant; ex hoc respectu (ideò) est, (quod) τοῖς *mantrhai* τῶν *Beidha* vestigial (effectus) fiat. Et si vos etiam in opera τῶν Beidha vestrorum ipsorum initium τε *Athrban Beid* ingressum non facitis, opera vestra deficiens (opus) et sine vestigio est futurum: et opus faciens, et opus faciens facere destructus (male mulctatus) est futurus: *mantr* vestrum vestigium non est largiturum. Oportet, quod, filios vestros ipsum hoc edoceatis, [et natos filiorum vestrorum]. Si ipso hoc modo facitis, (liber) *Rak Beid*, et *Djedjr Beid*, et *Sam Beid*, sine vestigio non est futurus. οἱ *rek'heschiran* dixerunt: approbatum fecimus, o digne veneration! sine timore, et sine tristitia, et laeto statu redditi sunt. Ex hoc respectu (idcirco) omnes *Beid khanan* (τε Beid lectores) in principio τῶν manthrahi τε Beid, et operum τε Beid, sectionum τε Beid Beid, (scilicet, libri) *Rak Beid*, et Djedjr Beid, et Sam Beid, τo kalmeh magnum, Oum omnino (necessario) pronunciant." For a critical evaluation of Duperron's Oupnek'hat cf. App (2014).

own accord. This is what the creators of the Veds want when they teach us to pronounce OM: cum adkiteh, that is, with divine inwardness. (Krause 1891: 310)[17]

The ancient Brahmin doctrine further speaks of the way to attain knowledge of ultimate reality, and thereby union with ultimate reality, and of the utterance of the sacred name Om, which signifies ultimate reality, and it is of this that all the Ved's speak the most and in the greatest detail. (Krause 1821: 463).

2.3 Panentheism and the Vedic Traditions

Based on the hermeneutics of the primacy of knowledge, the primacy of God, the primacy of existential transformation, and the proper goal of life, Krause provides a panentheistic interpretation of the main teaching of the Vedas:

The Vedas contain the pure intuition (*die reine Wesenschauung*) of Essence [that is, God, Brahma, or the Absolute, BPG] and the universal recognition that everything that is—nature and man, body and mind—is in God, or rather, that God in Himself is everything that is; that God—that is, Essence (*Wesen*)—is present in everything, reigns in everything, guides and governs all life as a whole; that the souls of human beings are capable of becoming one with God, if they strive for the knowledge of God, if they grow inward and intimate with God, and imitate God by leading a pure moral life, behaving with others in a just, loving and peaceful manner, and without following the impulses of fear and hope and of pleasure and pain; if they become similar to God in knowledge, feeling, and willing in giving peace to all beings and loving even their enemies and persecutors. According to the explicit and repeated declarations of this ancient Indian teaching of the Vedas, the only means of union with God is the intuition of Essence (*Wesenschauung*) through true scientific knowledge and pure and unselfish virtue. But the Vedas recognize ignorance (*Unwissenheit*) as the first source of all

---

17 Krause here refers to the Mundaka-Upanishad Verse 3.2.9 as translated in the Oupnek'hat, Vol. 1, 393: "Quisquis illum *Brahm* intelligit, *Brahm* fit; id est, quisquis Deum intelligit, Deus fit." The explanation "quisquis Deum intelligit, Deus fit," which is not to be found in the Sanskrit-Original, indicates that Duperron had a theistic understanding of Brahman. This probably fitted well with Krause's panentheistic understanding of the Upanishads. For Krause, "Brahman" and "Or-Essence"—see below—probably would have been synonymous. Cf. According to Riedel (1954: 211), Krause was aware that the ancient Indian word "Om" is of special metaphysical significance: "The primal Indian word Om is the name for that which was, is and becomes, altogether. […] Krause emphasizes: 'The Brahmin therefore prescribe themselves divine inwardness: Not to pronounce God's name unless with a holy sense, with a pure mind that is above pleasure and pain and every longing, and to think about it seriously and sacredly.' "

perversion and evil—that is, the lack of the knowledge of God (*den Mangel an Gotterkenntniss*), which arises from the limitation to sensuality and the resultant distraction and carelessness. (Krause 1887: 39)[18]

Because Krause considered the Upaniṣads—to his knowledge, written in the sixth century BC—to be a collection of the purely metaphysical teaching of the Vedas, it comes as no surprise that on Krause's understanding, the Upaniṣads contain a panentheistic metaphysics as well:

> God is the One Being, the One that is; He has no opposition and is therefore not to be recognised and named according to any particular quality; He is neither merely the infinite, nor merely the finite, and neither mere doing, nor mere suffering; apart from Him there is nothing,—all that is finite exists through Him; and He Himself, the unnameable Essence, is present in all and rules in all in independent, free power, in goodness, in wisdom and in justice. Humanity's destiny and dignity is: to know God, to love God, to become similar to God, to be united with God in this life and beyond. Virtue is God-likeness, must be freely willed, independent of fear and hope, of reward and punishment. […] These are the basic truths of the Indian system, which are found quite clearly and definitely in the Oupnek'hat. (Krause 1885: 66–67)

In support of his panentheistic metaphysical interpretation of the Vedas and the Upanishads, Krause approvingly quotes the Isha-Upanishad, Verse 6–7:

> But he who sees all beings in the general spirit and in all beings the spirit will henceforth despise nothing. If for those who know all beings are only the spirit, what stupidity is there, what pain in him who sees the unity of things? (Krause 1887: 44 FN).

Krause here apparently quotes from Frank (1826: 33). However, the original German in Frank has "Blindheit"—"Blindness"—instead of "Blödheit"—"Stupidity"—as in Krause's quotation.

Krause himself claimed not to have been influenced by the Indian traditions in any substantial way:

> One cannot say that Indian absolutism was reborn in German absolutism; for one only became acquainted with the latter in Germany after Kant, Fichte and Schelling had already made their main works known; even Hegel's system proves to be independent of Indian absolutism. I too may confess that I owe my teaching in no way to Indian absolutism. (Krause 1834: 376)

---

18 Cf. also Krause (1843: 215): "A doctrine such as this: that humans living in intimacy with God should love all men as men, friends and enemies, blood relatives and strangers, and that he should give peace to all beings, such a doctrine will never fail to have a good effect; nor has it ever failed to do so in the peoples who live by the Brahmine faith."

However, Krause probably held the panentheism of the Vedas and the Upaniṣads in such high esteem because his own panentheism *nolens volens* is a modern expression of ancient Indian thought itself.

3. Krause's Panentheism

Krause, not Schelling, introduced the *terminus technicus* 'panentheism' into the philosophical debate, and thereby took up an idea that he saw already anticipated in the Vedic tradition. Krause's panentheism, which he also simply calls 'the teaching of Essence' (*Wesenlehre*), is a particular philosophy of the Absolute. Krause also calls the Absolute "God" or "Essence" (*Wesen*). Krause saw himself as a successor of Kant who, breathing the spirit of German idealism went, with Kant, beyond Kant, in that he subjected Kant's transcendental philosophy to a metaphysical re-reading, because according to his own assessment, in his panentheism Krause has solved the problem arising from Kant's philosophy of "whether the Ideas of Reason (*Vernunftideen*) are not related to the categories (*Kategorien*) (his highest concepts of the Understanding [*obersten Verstandesbegriffen*]) in the same way that the categories are related to sensuality" (Krause 1869: 228). Therefore, Krause (1890: 143/144) classifies his own work as follows:

> I can actually consider myself the first follower of Kant. But I became this originally, of my own accord, without intending to. For, what appears as a continuation of Kant was already largely completed in 1803, before I was able to fully understand the relationship between Kant's research and works and my own. At that time I had only read and thought through very little of Kant's writings. Rather, my system, which was already completed in its first principles and main teachings in the years 1805 and 1806, became the key to Kant's aspiration. And it makes it possible for me to understand Kant's project, and to appreciate it from the highest position.

Krause already formulated the guiding metaphysical principle of his theory of the Absolute in 1813, as follows:

> My main principle is that all Science (*Wissenschaft*) is based on the intuition (*Anschauung*) of an infinite substance. This intuition cannot be proven from the Principle of Sufficient Reason (*Satz des Grundes*), but may only be shown present (*vorhanden*) within the human spirit. Everything that is, is this substance and within this substance. And all scientific knowledge must equivalently be that primordial intuition (*Uranschauung*) itself, and within it (Hohlfeld and Wünsche 1903: 362–363)

Because proving something means "recognizing that its essence must be as it is in a higher whole" (Krause 1869: 12), a philosophical proof of the existence of the Absolute as a proof that the Absolute exists, is conceptually excluded: For the Absolute is conceived as the highest whole, outside of which there is nothing that could be used to prove its existence.

3.1 The Analytical and the Synthetic Part of Philosophy

Krause's entire theoretical program is a justification and explication of the monistic principle stated above. From an epistemological perspective, Krause deploys transcendental reflections to present the intuition (*Anschauung*) of the one infinite substance as an intellectual vision (*Schau*) of the Absolute. Krause primarily uses the concept of vision (*Schau*) and not the concept of intuition (*Anschauung*), because the concept of intuition suggests an external relation between the subject and the object of knowledge, which is not to be had in the panentheism to be developed, because, if it is true, everything is a metaphysical part of the Absolute:

> "Intuition" is not so good to use here as "vision", because, when intuiting, one thinks of a contrary-relatedness (*Gegenverhaltheit*) of the external relation (*Außenverhalt*) between the one who looks and what is seen. But this is not consistently the case. For example: In the vision of Essence (*bei der Schauung Wesens*), there is no external relation, external contrary-relation, but an internal-contrary-relation [presents itself]. (Krause 1892a: 109)

The vision of the Absolute, according to Krause, is in principle accessible to every human being, which is to say that every human, if properly transcendentally trained and philosophically educated, is able to immediately understand the fundamental nature of empirical reality, and the Absolute empirical reality is metaphysically grounded in:

> Every human being has the original concept of Essence (*Urbegriff von Wesen*) unconsciously in himself (Krause 1892a: 91)

However, every human being must execute this vision (*Schau*) for themselves:

> Everyone must find this fundamental vision (*Grundschauung*) within themselves. It could not be brought to them from outside. (Krause 1869: 49)

The vision of the Absolute is not only the vision of the fundamental ground of empirical reality, but precisely due to this it is at the same time the vision of the one all-encompassing principle of the System of Science (*System der Wissenschaft*) because the possibility of such an organic System of Science presupposes the existence of a unifying principle, which lies at the foundation of everything:

> Science [is] possible only when it is granted to human reason to recognize the one, infinite, unconditioned being (*das Eine, unendliche, unbedingte Wesen*) [i.e. to recognize the Absolute, BPG], in which is all that is; which is recognized as the one ground of everything finite (*der Eine Grund alles Endlichen*). (Krause 1893a: 72)

Therefore, he who has the intellectual vision of the Absolute is not only able to understand the form of the true System of Science but is also in a position to spell out the metaphysical foundation of the System of Science, which Krause plainly calls Fundamental Science (*Grundwissenschaft*). Because, as he says:

> Under the System of Science [...] the whole of knowledge is conceived, in which all particular items of knowledge (*Erkenntnisse*) are contained, as parts, connected with one another and with the whole. (Krause 1886: 1)

Krause calls the transcendental path to obtain this vision of the Absolute 'the analytical-ascending' (*analytisch-aufsteigende*) part of philosophy. It is the ultimate starting point for the development of the System of Science; the philosophical training and epistemological propaedeutics of Krause's metaphysics.

The analytical-ascending part of philosophy

> starts out from the first certain knowledge that is found in every consciousness [...] and constantly rises to higher and higher knowledge, until the discovery of the fundamental knowledge (*Grunderkenntnis*) [of the Absolute, BPG]. This must show itself on this way, if a System of Science is to be possible for the human mind. (Krause 1886: 4)

Because Krause assumed that the vision (*Schau*) of the Absolute is possible for every human being, the analytical-ascending part of philosophy includes

> the sense-distracted spirits (*sinnzerstreuten Geister*) of all, in each of their states, crude and educated peoples, children, adults and old men, male and female spirits. Then it grasps the sense-distracted human being purely as human being, as a spiritual human being (*als Geistmenschen*), in the spiritual state common to all pre-scientific human beings, as it were, on the ground and soil in which all differences in pre-scientific minds and moods take root, germinate, and grow. (Krause 1890: 39)

As soon as the analytical-ascending part of philosophy has reached its goal, that is, the human being has risen to the immediately certain vision of the Absolute as the all-encompassing principle of both empirical reality and the System of Science, the *synthetic-descending* (*synthetisch-absteigende*) part of philosophy follows. This has the following task:

> In and through the fundamental knowledge achieved, that is, in and through the Principle, to develop all particular and conditioned knowledge as an Organism (*Organismus*) [of philosophy] (Krause 1886: 4).

That is:

> Based on the knowledge and acknowledgment (*Erkenntnis und Anerkenntnis*) of the Principle, the only task of the whole of scientific education [would

> be] the development of all knowledge within the fundamental knowledge (*Grunderkenntnis*) of the Principle; the one thought (*der Eine Gedanke*): Infinite, unconditional Being (*Wesen*) unfolds within the finite spirit (*Geiste*), within an Organism of scientific thoughts. Therefore, just as everything that is, and lives, is in the One, so also all knowledge is, and lives, in the one knowledge of the One (*in der einen Erkenntnis des Einen*). (Krause (1869: 20)

Because transcendental reflection, according to Krause, enables profound metaphysical insights into the nature of ultimate reality—because the analytical-ascending part of philosophy culminates in and enables the synthetic-descending part of philosophy—metaphysics and transcendental philosophy mutually complement and enrich each other: The synthetic deduction of the System of Science always remains bound to its origin in the transcendental reflections of the Ego, which serve as a corrective to purely conceptual deductions:

> When the principle is recognized, the content of the analytical part is by no means rejected, corrected, refuted, but rather recognized in the light of the principle. In this way, the first analytical part of philosophy does not grow up like useless seed husks or leaf fronds (*Keimblätter oder Blatthüllen*), to afterwards fall off. But it remains the same as the lower root and as the first branches of this tree of philosophy, within the finite spirit (*im endlichen Geiste*). […] What is found analytically remains eternally true, and then enters into the whole System of Synthetic Science as a subordinate part. (Krause (1869: 21)

In regard to the analytical-ascending part of philosophy as a necessary element of the complete system of philosophy, that is, in regard to the procedure to start metaphysics with a proper reflection concerning the nature of the Ego before turning to the nature of the Absolute, Krause sees himself as standing in a long philosophical tradition which unfortunately has been neglected in post-Kantian philosophy:

> Historically, I notice that our analytical part of philosophy is sought after by several thinkers, suspected, and even partly formulated in certain initial points. In the succession of Hellenic thinkers, Socrates sensed the essential nature of this rise of the finite spirit to a principle when he demanded: *Know yourself. And, only once strengthened by self-knowledge, undertake to know God, and things outside of you.* Similarly Kant, who compares himself to Socrates in this very respect […]. Since then, however, the main analytical part has been missing in all systems of philosophy, including all German. (Krause 1869: 22)

3.2 The Thought of the Absolute

Krause begins the analytical-ascending part of philosophy with phenomenological reflections pertaining to the nature of the pre-reflective Ego and, reminiscent of Husserl's *epochē*, brackets all knowledge that from a phenomenological point of view is not immediately certain:

> The analytical part does not drift about in all sorts of hypotheses and desultorous reasonings, but grasps the first certainty of the consciousness of the spirit (*das erste Gewisse des Bewusstseins des Geistes*). All assumptions, all hypotheses, all unauthorized musings are kept out of the analytical way. There is also no talk of what we feel, believe, mean, wish, hope, but only of what we already recognize: know (*erkennen—wissen*). (Krause 1869: 20)

Bracketing all mediated knowledge, the Ego thus is the transcendental principle of its own essence. For, it becomes conscious of itself, through itself:

> The Ego is itself the principle of its self-knowledge. And in the fundamental vision: I (*Grundschauung: Ich*) everything that the Ego contains in and of itself (*an und in sich*), all inner (immanent) ((*innerliche (immanente*)) knowledge of the Ego is also jointly contained, jointly given, jointly founded (*mit enthalten, mitgegeben, mitbegründet*). And, for precisely that reason, we [...] appreciated that the possibility is now open to us to develop the *self-science* (*Selbstwissenschaft*) of the Ego in its inner depth. (Krause 1869: 254)

3.2.1 The Ego as a Self-Same and Whole Being

The first and fundamental phenomenological insight into one's own nature is the realization that the Ego initially recognizes itself as a unity (*Einheit*), independently of any further determination:

> The first thing by which we recognize ourselves, that which we find ourselves as, is: as one being (*als Was wir uns finden, ist: als Ein Wesen*). (Krause 1869: 210)

That is:

> When it is said that I am one (*dass Ich Eins bin*), that is not just to be understood as a number, i.e. that the I is not two, not three, not four, etc., but by it is meant the unity of the essence itself (*es ist damit gemeint die Einheit der Wesenheit selbst*). (Krause 1869: 68)

The unity of the essence of the Ego, according to Krause, shows itself as the unity of a plurality of further determinations. Looking purely at itself, the Ego finds that it cannot think of its unity without understanding itself as a *self-same* and a *whole* being:

> We cannot think of ourselves [...] as one, without thinking of ourselves as the same, and as a whole (*als Selbes und als Ganzes*). (Krause 1869: 211)
> Task: to fulfill the vision (*Schauung*): what the Ego is in itself; or: to grasp the fundamental essence (*Grundwesenheit*) of the Ego in pure observation. Result: the Ego is a being (*Wesen*), and indeed a self-same, whole being (*ein selbes, ganzes Wesen*). (Krause 1886: 17)

On the one hand, that the Ego is a *self-same* being denotes the property that the Ego "is what it is, not through (*durch*) any relation, or in (*in*) any relation, but in itself (*an sich*)" (Krause 1869: 68).[19] On the other, that the Ego shows itself in self-observation as a *whole* being means that the Ego is the totality of its intrinsic determinations.[20] The *wholeness* of the Ego is thus the reverse side of its *self-sameness*: While self-sameness emphasizes the substantiality of the Ego, wholeness focuses on emphasizing the intrinsic self-reliance of the Ego as a whole prior to, and over and above, its determinations. The Ego is therefore neither a bundle of its properties nor a *substratum* devoid of properties.

3.2.2 The Ego as Body and Spirit

That the Ego cannot grasp itself transcendentally without presupposing that it is a self-same and a whole being, however, is only the first step on the analytical-ascending path of philosophy. Based on this insight, the Ego is able to further specify, from a phenomenological point of view, its appearance as a self-same and whole being:

> In my independence as I (*Selbstständigkeit als Ich*) is included my independence as spirit (*Geist*), then my independence as body (*Leib*), finally my united independence, whereby I am an independent being made up of spirit and body united. (Krause 1869: 103)

If the Ego recognizes itself phenomenologically as body (*Leib*), then it at once recognizes that it always already understands its body as part of Nature, which encompasses the body. As Krause (1869: 84) says:

> We claim that the whole body is formed by Nature; that it is, and persists, in Nature, that it is created, that it is born, that it grows, that it decreases, that it decays. These are all actions of Nature. Therefore, in this respect, the body belongs to Nature rather than to Spirit.

If the Ego recognizes itself as Spirit (*Geist*), it recognizes itself as part of an encompassing realm of Reason or Spirit. Finally, if the Ego recognizes itself as a union of Nature and Reason, then it recognizes itself as a human being:

> The Ego therefore finds itself as Spirit, and in the sense mentioned as body, and as the essential union (*Vereinwesen*) of both, i.e. as human being. (Krause 1869: 180)

---

19 See also Krause (1869: 70): "We have found that the Ego recognizes itself as an independent being (*selbstständiges Wesen*), as one essential self (*als Ein Selbwesen*). For that you usually need the word 'substance' (*Substanz*)."
20 Cf. Krause (1869: 70): "That the Ego is whole, is usually denoted by the word 'totality.'"

According to Krause, the fact that Nature and Reason may be reconciled in human beings is grounded in the fact that Nature and Reason indeed differ in essence, but are always already mediated by each other:

> Nature, therefore, insofar as it is rational (organic), is in Reason and is incorporated (*aufgenommen*) into Reason. [...] But Reason, insofar as it is natural, is in Nature and is incorporated into Nature in so far as Nature is Reason. (Krause 2007: 81/82)

For Krause, Reason and Nature thus are distinguishable, but absolutely equally valuable determinations of the human being: The Ego participates in Reason through spirit, in Nature through the body, and as a human being it finds itself as a being in which Nature and Reason are always already mediated.[21] For Krause (1869: 104) it was of great importance that the Ego as spirit is not axiologically superior to the Ego as body:

> And as far as the relation of this teaching to life is concerned, it is of the greatest practical importance how the relation of the spirit to the body appears to the human being. For example, if the human being thinks of the spirit as being of the same essence as the body, then they will also respect the body as something essential, worthy in itself. They will take care of the body, protect it, develop it, and try to keep it healthy and beautiful. On the other hand, if someone is of the opinion that the spirit is not at all independent, but only a specific activity of the body, perhaps only the highest animal function, then they will easily fall into the opinion that if the body dies, so it is with the spirit, and, for just that reason, the human being is only obliged to mainly and primarily care for their body.

3.2.3 The Ego is not the Absolute

The phenomenological insight that the Ego participates both in Reason and Nature and finds Nature and Reason mediated in its own being, according to Krause, yields a central insight for the further course of the analytical-ascending part of philosophy, namely that the Ego is *not* the Absolute, therefore is not itself the one all-encompassing principle of the System of Science. This is because, although the Ego is the principle of its own being, the Ego does neither reveal itself phenomenologically as the all-encompassing principle of science nor as a self-sufficient being that can account for its own existence and suchness:

---

21 See Hofmann (1988: 270): "Taking up Plato, Thomas Aquinas, Spinoza and Leibniz and thus going back earlier than Kant, Krause regards Spirit and Nature in his [philosophy], in contradiction with Hegel, as equally essential fundamental beings."

> Can then the fundamental vision: I (*Grundschauung: Ich*) also contain everything that is in any way thinkable [?] For, we say [...] that only that which is everything essentially as such and in itself (*alles Wesenlich an sich und in sich*), and has nothing outside of itself, may be the unconditional principle [of philosophy]. Therefore, if the thought: I (*der Gedanke: Ich*) is to be the One Principle of Science (*Wissenschaft*), its content, the I, must be everything that is. It must be the one being (*das Eine Wesen sein*). But is that then found in the fundamental vision: I? I don't find it asserted in any way. (Krause 1869: 56)

Furthermore:

> If the fundamental vision: I were the Principle [of the one whole Science], then this thought: I would have to be sufficient for itself (*sich selbst genügen*): No other thought at all would need to be possible, for I. For, even the thought of anything other than the Ego is the Ego's indication that the thought of the Ego does not involve all thoughts. Accordingly, the fundamental vision: I, can by no means be regarded as the Principle of the one whole Science (*Wissenschaft*). (Krause 1889: 56)

Because, however, in phenomenological reflection, the Ego understands itself quite concretely by the different dimensions of its existence as a body, as a spirit, and as a human being, the question arises for the Ego as to the ground for the conditions of the possibility of its being. Since the Ego does not sufficiently encompass Nature or Spirit in such a way that it could bring about this synthesis of Nature and Spirit itself, and since, as its *relata*, neither Nature nor Reason may bring about this synthesis, the Ego that has become conscious of itself as a human being—firmly deploying the principle of sufficient reason—faces the question of the ontological ground of Nature, Reason, and their unification, to form humanity. It faces the question of the ground *in virtue of which* its being and its essence as a human being are made possible and actual:

> So where does this union of spirit and body come from[?] And why is this union with Nature so determinate and limited[?] It is obvious that these important questions cannot be answered from our present position (*jetzigen Standorte*). For they raise themselves above (*erheben sich über*) the realm of determinate inner perception. We have just now become conscious that Spirit (*Geist*) is not the cause of the subsistence (*Bestehens*) of this wonderful relation. But what the cause of it actually is, may only be found if we are able to rise (*erheben*) above body and above spirit. (Krause 1869: 112)

That is:

> We cannot avoid asking about the ground of Reason, Nature and humanity. That is, we must rise to the thought of a being (*zu dem Gedanken eines Wesens erheben*) in which both Reason and Nature are incorporated (*enthalten seien*), that whereby, that is, according to its essence (*Wesenheit*), these two are determined (*bestimmt seien*): that which is also the ground for the union of both, according to which they are humanity (*die Menschheit*). (Krause 1869: 204)

3.2.4 The Concept of the World and the Absolute as the Ultimate Ground of the World

The thought of a being which is the ground of the union of Spirit and Nature, according to Krause, is a thought developed purely transcendentally through phenomenological reflections on the nature of the Ego. The Ego has shown itself thus (a) as participating both in the realm of Spirit and Nature, and (b) as a human being in which Spirit and Nature are always already mediated. Against this background, Krause claims that the thought of the being in which the union of Spirit and Nature is grounded is in fact identical with the thought of the all-encompassing principle of science. To shows this, Krause first argues that Nature and Reason, although infinite in a certain way, are not absolutely infinite. The fact that Nature is not Reason is sufficient to show that, in Krause's system, Reason, Nature, and thus humanity are, seen absolutely, finite realms of being:

> We have thought of Reason as infinite in its way. But, because it is not Nature, because by itself it is not humankind either, Reason is nevertheless thought as finite in this respect. In the same way, of course, we also thought of Nature as infinite in its way, as infinite in space, in time, and with regard to strength. But it is not Spirit, [not] Reason, it is also not humanity on its own. Therefore, it is also thought to be finite and limited in this respect. (Krause 1869: 203)

Krause then goes on to argue that Nature, Reason, and humanity constitute what is adequately designated as "the world":

> By the word "world" [is signified] both Nature, infinite in its kind, and Reason, infinite in its kind, as well as humanity, infinite in its kind. For, even if these three beings, each of its kind, are infinite, they are nevertheless finite […] because each of them, as such, is not what each other, as such, is (*ein Jedes davon, als solches, nichts ist, Was ein jedes Andere, als solches, ist*). (Krause 1828: 305)

Deploying this concept of the world, it follows that the thought of the being that grounds Nature, Reason, and humanity is identical with the thought of the constitutive ground of the world. In a second step, Krause argues that the concept of the world is identical with the concept of the realm of finitude:

> As far as […] the intuition (*Schauung*) world is concerned: This is usually defined as the entirety of everything finite (*Inbegriff von allem Endlichen*), or as the totality of finite beings (*das Ganze aller endlichen Wesen*), or as the aggregate of things (*die Gesamtheit der Dinge*). So the world is not thought of as originally a whole, prior to and above all parts, in essential unity, that is in essence-unity (*in Wesenheit-Einheit*), but only as a union of the finite (*ein Vereinganzes des Endlichen*). (Krause 1828: 305)

Because, according to Krause, there is nothing finite in any respect that may not be subordinated to Nature, Reason, or humanity, it follows that the world as constituted by Nature, Reason, and humanity is the entirety of finitude. Therefore, based on Krause's concept of the world, it follows that the thought of the ground of Spirit, Nature, and the union of Spirit and Nature *ipso facto* is the thought of the ground of the entirety of finitude, and thereby the thought of the all-encompassing, that is, unconditional and infinite principle of philosophy. Finally, because the thought of the Absolute is the thought of this all-encompassing principle, the thought of that in which Spirit, Nature, and their union as humanity, are metaphysically grounded, is nothing but the thought of the Absolute itself. Formulated *ex negativo*: If this thought were not the thought of the unconditional and infinite supreme being, it would not be able to provide the ultimate grounding of Nature, Reason, and humanity that Krause was looking for. This is because it would itself, according to the Principle of Sufficient Reason, imply the question of its ground. Therefore, in Krause's system, the groundless ground may only be the thought of the one, unconditional, and infinite being (*Wesens*):

> Does this being (*Wesen*), as we think it, itself have a higher ground (*Grund*)? If we think of it as finite, if we think that it too has something else outside of it, then we must again ask about the higher ground of this being, which we think of as the ground of Reason, Nature, and humanity. (Krause 1869: 204)

3.2.5 The Infinite and Unconditioned Absolute

As the thought of the all-encompassing principle of philosophy, the thought of the Absolute is, in its content, infinite and unconditional:

> Therefore, whoever thinks this thought purely and clearly must also think that there is nothing whatsoever outside of this being (*Wesen*). From the other side, however, in this thought, it is thought that the infinite being contains everything finite that is there. For, because there is nothing outside of it, and because finitude *is*, as we know with immediate certainty, everything finite can only be thought of as being (*seyend*) in the one unconditional, infinite, being (*Wesen*) that is thought (*gedacht*). Therefore, since the one infinite being is thought of as everything determinate as being in itself (*in sich seyend*), it is thought of as the one ground of all finite things; therefore also as the one ground of the world, as the one ground of Reason, Nature, and humanity. (Krause 1836: 407)

The thought of the Absolute entails that everything finite that the Ego is able to recognize is itself contained in the thought of the Absolute, and is recognized as being contained in it: Whatever the object of its thought, when the Ego recognizes it, it recognizes it not only as *ontologically* grounded in and through the Absolute, but also as *epistemologically* included in the thought of the Absolute. For everything finite and conditioned is only what it is through its unconditional and infinite ground:

> For whatever finite, definite, thing may be thought of, its object (*dessen Gegenstand*) cannot be thought outside of God, but as within God, as grounded and determined through God. *Therefore, all finite specific thoughts, including the thought: I, are contained in this one essence-thought (diesem Einen Wesengedanken) or God thought (Gottgedanken)*. (Krause 1836: 410)

That is to say, if the thought of the Absolute is more than a thought, if the thought of the Absolute is indeed the self-indication of the Absolute, then there is no object of reference outside of the Absolute. Everything that the Ego can know, everything that is, is then the one infinite and unconditional Absolute, and the finite constituted in and through it:

> [It] follows at the same time that God is also thought of uniquely and alone (*einzig und allein*) as the one and whole ground of all knowledge (*Grund aller Erkenntnis*), as the one knowledge-ground (*der Eine Erkenntnisgrund*); in the first place, therefore, as the ground of the self-knowledge of the Ego. […] At the same time, God is further thought of as the ground of all knowledge of the self that exceeds the self (*aller äußern das Ich übersteigenden Erkenntnis des Ich*), indeed, as we saw, in the first place as the knowledge-ground [of the facts] that I can myself think of God, and that the Ego can also think God as the Ground of the Ego and of all knowledge […] but then also as ground of all knowledge by the Ego of finite beings (*Wesen*), that are outside the Ego. (Krause 1869: 261/262)

3.3 The Vision of the Absolute

However, whether the developed thought of the Absolute entails the reality of the Absolute, that is, whether the Ego is authorized to interpret its thought of the Absolute as an immediately certain self-revelation of the Absolute, has not yet been decided on the analytical-ascending path of philosophy. To show that the thought of the Absolute is in fact the self-revealing vision of the Absolute, that is, to foster our insight that the thought of the Absolute guarantees its own validity in and through itself, Krause turns to an analysis of the concept of recognition:

> I use the word: 'recognition' (*Erkennen*), in a quite general and comprehensive sense, to denote any presence of any essence (*Wesenlichen*), or of any object (*Gegenstandes*), in consciousness. This presence might now be perfect and complete or it might still be inadequate and incomplete. When a being's presence in consciousness is complete, we usually use the word 'knowledge' (*Wissen*). If, however, this presence of an object in consciousness is not yet complete, still imperfect, then we use various other words, e.g. 'suspicion', 'belief', 'guesswork', 'opinion' (*Ahnen, Glauben, Vermuten, Meinen*). (Krause 1869: 112)

Because recognition denotes the presence of an object in consciousness in varying degrees, the concept of recognition is tripartite:

> In recognition, there is a relation between the recognizing being and the recognized being (*das erkennende Wesen und das erkannte Wesen*). […] And I distinguish

these two, which stand in this relation to one another, from the content of the relation itself, namely, from recognition. [...] We have to distinguish three things in this relation of recognition: the recognizing, the recognized, and the recognition (*das Erkennende, das Erkannte und die Erkenntnis*). (Krause 1869: 186)[22]

Krause understands the differing degrees of recognition, and the process of recognizing, within the framework of a correspondence theory of truth, because "what is true must be thought of as it is in itself, so that [in] knowledge, the presentation of the object (*die Vorstellung des Gegenstandes*) agrees with the object itself" (Krause 1869: 6). Krause thus was aware that truth understood in terms of the coherence theory is not sufficient to constitute Science:

> If science is to be science (namely science in general), then it must be systematic. However, this alone does not comprise science. For there might be formed, on some presupposition of an unproven assumption, a systematic sequence of inferences, a structure of elements, and yet it is not knowledge (*Wissen*); because even error (*Irrtum*) can be consistent. (Krause 1892a: 53)

Against this background, for Krause, recognition thus specified, is not, as with Kant, transcendentally incapable of recognizing things-in-themselves, but is aimed straightforwardly at recognizing things as they are, even when they are not objects of recognition:

> We find that knowing as independent (*Selbständiges*) is related with the known as independent; indeed, in such a way that both likewise obtain (*bestehen*) within knowledge as independent, and yet are related. Or in other words, the knowing and the known are united in knowledge as self-essentials (*Selbwesenliche*), so that they obtain as self-essentials. [...] And if I recognize something that is outside of me [...] then I again distinguish myself as that independent from those recognized things, also as independent. And they are united in knowledge as independent, with me as independent: They do not pass over into me (*sie gehen nicht in mich über*), do not give up their independence in mine. They remain, recognized by me, as independent as if I did not recognize them, and yet they are united with me in knowledge. (Krause 1869: 190–191)

Thus, Krause's concept of recognition, in a first step, entails that for recognition to be possible at all, the recognizing subject and the recognized object have to be properly united: The recognized object has to be present in consciousness. While the Ego is what enables any recognition concerning the

---

22 In places, Krause's epistemology is reminiscent of scholastic reflections on the subject. Krause held the philosophy of the Middle Ages in high esteem: "The philosophy of the Middle Ages is far from being as well known and appreciated as it deserves. One has misconstrued the form of the content, like the mineralized metal in the ore. And even the form and its linguistic representation has not been rightly appreciated" (Krause 1829: 303).

Ego itself—the Ego as recognizing subject and at once as recognized object is itself the uniting principle of any recognition pertaining to the Ego—any object of recognition that transcends the realm of the phenomenological self-observation of the Ego presupposes something beyond the Ego to unite it with the Ego, that is, something which is the ground of the presence of this object in consciousness:

> For every thought that transcends the Ego, a thought of an external ground with regard to the Ego be must be accepted. This then applies to every thought that exceeds the Ego, whether that thought is of something finite and conditioned, or infinite and unconditioned. (Krause 1869: 255/256)

Because the thought of the unconditioned and infinite Absolute, as shown, is a thought that transcends the Ego, it follows that "this assertion is most valid with regard to the thought of the unconditional, infinite being or God, awakened above" (Krause 1869: 256).

Because the analytical-ascending part of philosophy has already shown that the thought of the all-encompassing Absolute is present in consciousness, it follows that there is something beyond the Ego that already united the thought of the Absolute with the Ego—that brought this thought into consciousness—and that the Ego knows about this. This something, however, can only be the Absolute itself. In other words, the thought of the Absolute could not be thought at all, if it were not always already the self-revelation of the infinite being in the finite consciousness of the Ego:

> When we are conscious of this thought: [...] God, we are at the same time conscious that this thought, even as our thought, cannot be grounded and caused by ourselves, nor by any other finite being, but that the possibility and the reality of this thought of ours can only be thought of as being based on the content of this thought, through Essence or God himself (*durch Wesen oder Gott selbst*). (Krause 1869: 256)

Furthermore:

> The thought: *God*, even as a thought, is not to be explained by any means through a *finite* I, or spirit. For, nothing is more comprehensible from its essence (*Wesenheit*) than that it is conscious of itself as I. Therefore, God himself is the teacher of anyone who has legitimately gleaned (*gesammelt*) spirit in itself, and in God, out of the sensory distraction (*Zerstreutheit*). (Krause 1836: 412–413)[23]

---

23 See also Wollgast (1990: 22): "Human self-knowledge, and therefore all knowledge, presupposes an absolute principle that makes the unity of thinking and being (*Sein*) possible in the first place. The subject searching for indubitable

3.4 The Absolute and the Principle of Sufficient Reason

The analytical-ascending part has reached its goal: Through phenomenological self-observation the Ego discovered that it always already possessed the thought of the Absolute, a thought it could not have if this thought was not at once the self-revelation of the one infinite und unconditioned Absolute. As a consequence, the Ego now is able to locate its thinking and being, as well as the world itself, ontologically and epistemologically in the Absolute.

However, there is one last point that needs clarification: The Ego deployed the Principle of Sufficient Reason to develop the thought of that which is the constitutive ground of the world:

> Now, we have been induced here to the accomplishment of this thought [of God, BPG] by the Principle of Sufficient Reason, in that we apply it to the three highest objects: Reason, Nature, and humanity. (Krause 1869: 205)

Now that the Ego has knowledge of the Absolute, the Ego can see that the Principle of Sufficient Reason itself is grounded in and through the Absolute:

> Now, however, the Principle of Sufficient Reason [...] itself is something definitely finite [...]. Consequently, even by the Principle of Sufficient Reason, this principle must also be applied to itself. The reason for the reason (*Grunde des Grundes*) must be asked for, the why of the why, the through of the through (*es muss nach dem Grunde des Grundes gefragt werden, nach dem Warum des Warum, nach dem Durch des Durch*). (Krause 1869: 259)

In other words, the ground of the validity of the Principle of Sufficient Reason, and therefore the ground of the intelligibility of reality, can be none other than the Absolute itself:

> How did we arrive at the thought of unconditional, infinite being? [...] It seems that we arrived at this thought by means of the concept and Principle of Sufficient Reason. But "by means of", does not mean "through". And it is evident that we were prompted by this thought to become aware (*inne zu werden*) of the thought: God. But our inner perception (*innere Wahrnehmung*) does not at all contain this, the thought: Ground itself might be the ground of the thought: God. [...] Rather the other way around, just as we become conscious of the thought: God, and think this thought quite purely and correctly, we find that this thought is the fundamental thought (*Grundgedanke*) of our entire consciousness, and that also the property of being a reason (*Grund zu sein*), is subordinated within the thought of Essence or God (*Wesen oder Gott*). (Krause 1869: 258)

---

knowledge (*Wissen*), and thereby reflecting on itself, presupposes the Absolute, recognizes that it finds itself all along within the Absolute, that it can only recognize itself and the Absolute through the Absolute."

> Because this thought: Essence or God (*Wesen oder Gott*) as the thought of the one being (*des einen Wesens*) is unconditional, infinite, and in unconditional being-there-ness (*Daseinheit*), it may only be thought according to the concept and Principle of Sufficient Reason. Other than that, this thought is caused by itself, in and by the content (*Inhalt*) of that thought, by being or God Himself. (Krause 1869: 256)

The Principle of Sufficient Reason thus is part of the *ratio cognoscendi* of the Absolute. But the Absolute is the *ratio essendi* of the Principle of Sufficient Reason:

> As soon as the finite spirit has come to recognize the thought: Essence or God as the fundamental truth, it would also have the thought: ground, and, similarly, the thought of the ground of the ground. That is, the universal validity of the Principle of Sufficient Reason is also to be recognized and to be acknowledged (*erkennbar und anerkennbar*). For when the Absolute (*Wesen*) is thought as being everything by and in itself (*als alles an und in sich seiend*), it is thought as the ground of everything. And, consequently, the Principle of Sufficient Reason applies to everything determinately finite. And the fundamental thought is therefore: Essence or God is also, at the same time, the ground of authority of the very general applicability of the Principle of Sufficient Reason to everything that is finite in some respect according to some essence. (Krause 1869: 300)

Because, in fact, Krause begins the justification of his system of philosophy with the assumption that, based on the Principle of Sufficient Reason, empirical reality is a consistent and intelligible whole constituted by Nature and Spirit, and, in the end, grounds this consistency on the Absolute he thus discovered, one may *prima facie* argue that Krause is arguing in a circle. According to Krause, this is indeed the case, but his circle, however, is not a *vicious* one, but belongs to the very nature of philosophical reflection:

> You will object to me that my philosophy turns in a circle. I know this. It ought to be like this, and cannot be otherwise. The circle itself is the following: In order to philosophize one must have the belief, indeed the firm conviction, that the whole world is consistent, and if one has philosophized one comes back to the same thing (*dasselbe*) from which one started. Above all, it is to be noted that what is true, is that without which the human being cannot exist. If the latter is so, the truth (*das Wahre*) must be laid down in everyone, even the most uneducated person, perhaps in a peculiar form, because he cannot live without it. So it is no wonder that at the beginning of philosophy one cannot doubt what one only knows more certainly at the end of it. (Krause 1889: 66)

3.5 The Absolute as the One, Whole and Independent Being

The path of the analytical-ascending part of philosophy has come to an end. The synthetical-descending part of science now has the task to develop and to make explicit the System of Science based on the obtained vision of the Absolute:

> Based on the knowledge and acknowledgment of the fundamental principle, the elaboration of all knowledge is the only task of the whole of scientific culture. The one thought, the infinite, unconditioned *Essence*, unfolds itself in the finite mind in an organism of scientific thought, so that just as everything that exists and lives is in the One, so also all knowledge lives in the one knowledge of the One. (Krause 1869: 20)

A main task of the synthetic-descending part of philosophy is to clarify God's relation to the world. Because the world is the realm of the finite and conditioned, and because the Absolute has been recognized as the one unconditional and infinite being, Krause can, on the one hand, rule out *pantheism* as a suitable philosophical metaphysics, because it leads to a contradictory identification of the finite with the infinite (or of the conditioned with the unconditioned). But precisely because the Absolute is viewed as an infinite and unconditional being, Krause may also rule out *theism* as an adequate philosophical paradigm. This is because theism would contradict the unconditionality and infinity of the Absolute, through the ontological distinction between God and world: If the world were to stand "outside of" the Absolute, ontologically and epistemologically—i.e., if it were understandable from within itself in its being and suchness—it would be the abolition of the infinity and unconditionality of the Absolute as the all-encompassing principle of reality.

However, both pantheism and theism are right insofar as: On the one hand, there is, or can be thought of, nothing outside of God. And, on the other hand, the world as the embodiment of Nature, and Spirit, and the humanity constituted from both, is not self-explanatory and therefore requires an absolute ground. Therefore, the only adequate ontological framework for the System of Science (*System der Wissenschaft*), according to Krause is, *panentheism*: Panentheism dialectically mediates between pantheism and theism, and locates the world ontologically and epistemologically within the Absolute, without reducing the Absolute to the world:

> In the vision of Essence this is also found: that Essence, as the One, is also as such, or in itself, under itself, and through itself, everything (*auch an sich, oder in sich, unter sich, und durch sich Alles*), also the essence of everything finite. Therefore, the statement made according to this insight must be: that the One in itself and through itself is also the All (*dass das Eine in sich und durch sich auch das All sei*) […]. And, because in the vision of Essence (*Wesenschauung*) it is recognized that God is also everything in and through itself, Science (*Wissenschaft*) could well be called "panentheism." (Krause 1869: 313)

To spell out his panentheistic metaphysics, Krause once more turns to the concept of the infinite and unconditioned Absolute and analyzes both the semantic content of (a) the concept of infinity and (b) the concept of unconditionality.

(a) According to Krause, the concept of infinity *prima facie* only denotes the negation of finitude. *Secunda facie*, however, the concept of finitude itself is also to be understood as a negative term, because the concept of finitude implies that that which is finite has something outside of itself, to which it is related, and is therefore *not* the whole of which it is part. The concept of infinity is therefore a doubly negating concept which, positively speaking, expresses the determination of being a whole: "If we deny finitude [of the Absolute], then we find that this is the one whole, that is, that wholeness itself is infinity" (Krause 1828: 366). As Krause (1836: 409) clarifies: "It was found that the whole itself, as a whole, is the infinite. So instead of saying: 'the infinite being' (*das unendliche Wesen*), we may say: 'the whole being' (*das ganze Wesen*). However, this property: to be whole, must by no means be thought of as being bound up with limits but, rather, in such a way that there is absolutely nothing essential *outside of* this whole; just as space is whole in its own way, has no boundary around it, hence nothing similar, that is, no space out of itself." The Absolute, therefore, insofar as it is the one *infinite* being, is the one *whole* being. Consequently, all finite beings are (metaphysical) parts of this whole or, in Krause's terminology, 'partial wholes' (*Teilganze*).

(b) Krause proceeds analogously with the unconditionality (*Unbedingtheit*) of the Absolute: This term *prima facie* expresses the negation of conditionality. But the concept of being conditioned itself is a negative term. Because "something is conditioned [...] insofar as its essence is determined by something else outside of it" (Krause 1836: 409). The concept of conditionality therefore entails that that which is conditioned is what it is *not* on its own. The doubly negative concept of unconditionality is therefore, positively speaking, synonymous with the concept of independence: "If we look closely at what is signified by the denial of conditionality, we find that this is pure selfhood (*reine Selbheit*). To be purely the same (*rein Dasselbe sein*), without reference to the outside, that is unconditionality or independence" (Krause 1828: 366). The unconditionality of the Absolute is its independence. Because independence is understood by Krause as the absence of conditions, the unconditionality of the Absolute is its absolute freedom.[24]

---

24 See also Krause (1836: 409): "Instead of 'unconditionality', we must use the affirmative expression: 'sameness or selfhood, independence' (*Selbheit oder Selbstheit, Selbständigkeit*)."

Understanding infinity as wholeness, and unconditionality as independence, enables Krause to subject the *prima facie* negatively formulated vision of the Absolute—the Absolute seen as the one, infinite and unconditional being—to a hermeneutical re-reading and to reformulate it in the synthetic-descending part of philosophy as follows:

> Therefore, instead of saying, we think the one, infinite, unconditional being, we can more correctly say *purely affirmatively*: we think the one, the same, whole being, or: we think God according to His unity, sameness, wholeness. (Krause 1836: 409)

Finally, this knowledge about the opposing and yet united determinations of sameness and wholeness, as the highest determinations of the unity of the Absolute, according to Krause, corresponds precisely to the knowledge gained in the analytical-ascending part of philosophy about Spirit and Nature as the highest constituents of the world. In fact, on the one hand, Krause argues that the concept of sameness/selfhood designates that which is recognized as Spirit or Reason, because self-sameness is the defining mark of Reason and Spirit. On the other hand, Krause argues that the concept of wholeness refers to what the concept of Nature designates, because wholeness is the defining mark of Nature.[25] Based on the identification of selfhood (*Selbheit*) and Reason, as well as wholeness and Nature, Krause is able to conclude that the world, ultimately, is constituted by sameness (= Reason) and wholeness (= Nature). Because humanity in turn is the supreme union of Nature and Reason, that is, the supreme union of sameness and wholeness, it furthermore follows that *qua* participation in the sameness and wholeness of the Absolute, the essence of humanity is part of the essence of the Absolute.

3.6 Panentheism, Mereology and the Priority of the Whole

If the Absolute is the one, the same, and whole being, then it follows, according to Krause, that the world, and therefore everything finite, is ultimately grounded ontologically and epistemologically in the Absolute, and is thereby essentially similar to it. It also follows that the world, being grounded and limited by the Absolute, must, at the same time, be a metaphysical part of the Absolute and as such a relational-intrinsic determination of it. With regard to the Ego, Krause clarifies this as follows:

---

25 In Krause's (1828: 398) words: "[We find] that in the essence (*Wesenheit*) [...] of Reason, sameness is the determining, the predominating, the alone-self-essential (*Allein-Eigenwesenliche*) in the relation between sameness and wholeness. In Nature, on the other hand, it is wholeness that appears to us."

> Similarly, when it is asserted "The Ego, or every finite rational being (*Vernunftwesen*), is in God" this assertion means the following: God is also the Ego, also all Egos, but only as a part. The whole of God is not a finite Ego, nor all finite Egos. It is further thought that the Ego is of the same pure essence (*Wesenheit*) as Essence (*Wesen*), so that the Ego is one self-same and whole being (*Wesen*), as God is, but finite and limited, not infinite, as God is. (Krause 1828: 307/308)

In order to be able to capture this relationship between, on the one hand, the Absolute as the one, the self-same and whole being and, on the other hand, the world as a relational-intrinsic determination of the Absolute, constituted and grounded by the Absolute, Krause develops an organic metaphysical mereology in the synthetical-descending part of philosophy.

The central mereological assumption, which follows from Krause's panentheism, is that an organic whole has metaphysical priority over its parts, and their interrelationships. Such a whole is something in which all parts

> are with each other and persist, not just a whole in which parts stand side by side, [and] are combined into a mere aggregate. Rather, in such a whole, the parts are all in, with, and through each other, [and] are all only in, with, and through the whole. (Krause 1869: 4)

Based on the priority of the whole over its metaphysical parts, Krause distinguishes between five general mereological perspectives that may be adopted when considering a whole and its parts, as well as their mutual relations:

(1) *Anti-essential (Antwesenliche) Perspective*: When two opposing parts of a whole are considered, inasmuch as they are distinct parts of that whole, then that whole is considered *anti-essential* or as an *anti-essence* ("ant" is used here by Krause as a prefix indicating opposition, analogous to its use in the German word 'Antwort' (*answer*) which may be understood as a 'counter-word' (*Gegenwort*).

(2) *Mäl-essential perspective*: If two parts of a whole are considered insofar as they are constitutive of another part of the whole, then that whole is regarded as *mäl-essential* (mälwesenlich) or as a *Mälessence* (Mälwesen) ("mäl" is used analogously to its use in the German word *Vermählung* ('marriage') as a prefix indicating unity).

(3) *Om-essential perspective*: If all parts of a whole as well as all relations of all parts of a whole with other parts of this whole are considered, then that whole is regarded as *Om-essential* (omwesenlich) or an *Om-essence* (*Omwesen*). The totality of all parts of a whole, including all relations of all parts of a whole, is the 'organism' (*Gliedbau*) of this whole.

(4) *Or-essential Perspective*: When a whole is viewed as the whole that it is, including all of its parts, and the relations of all its parts, then it is considered *or-essential* (*orwesenlich*) or as an *or-essence* (*Orwesen*).
(5) *Ur-essential Perspective*: When a whole is viewed as the whole it is, without recourse to its parts and their relationships, then it is considered *ur-essential* or an *ur-essence*. The ur-essential perspective of a whole considers a whole insofar as it has metaphysical priority over its parts.[26]

Deploying these mereological neologisms, Krause is able to distinguish different perspectives on the Absolute and its relation to the world:

(1) Insofar as the world is thought of as a relational-intrinsic determination of the Absolute, the Absolute is thought of as the *Om-Essence*.
(2) Insofar as the Absolute is thought of as the one whole and self-same being, together with its parts and their relations, it is thought of as the *Or-Essence*. *Or-Essence* is the thought of the one, infinite and unconditioned being, together with its parts and their relations, outside of which there is nothing.
(3) If the Absolute is thought of as a whole that has metaphysical priority over its parts, then the Absolute is thought of as the *Ur-Essence*: "God is also Ur-Essence, i.e. God as a whole being is prior to, and over and above, all that God [i.e. Or-Essence, BPG] is in, under, and through itself" (Krause 1828: 310).

From the point of view of Krause's metaphysical mereology, *Or-Essence* and *Ur-Essence* must not be confused:

> Accordingly, if Or-Essence is called God, then the Absolute seen as Ur-Essence cannot simply and without any additions be referred to by the name of God as well. But it must then be said: God as Ur-Essence, or simply: Ur-Essence. (Krause 1828: 393)

Deploying the concepts of the different perspectives on the Absolute, Krause can clarify the dialectical relation between the world and the Absolute as follows. The fact that the world is *in* God means that it is what it is, because it is a metaphysical part of the Absolute:

> I use here […], following current usage, "in" of finite beings and essences (*Wesen und Wesenheiten*), and thereby indicate that the higher whole is this finite, as its part. Therefore, this finite part is the same as the whole in pure essence. However, it is limited in such a way that the limit of the finite is in common with its whole. But this limit does not limit or circumscribe the whole as a whole (*diese Grenze aber nicht das Ganze als Ganzes begrenzt oder umgrenzt*). (Krause 1869: 307)

---

26 Cf. Krause (1828: 310) and also Krause (1890: 42).

That the world is "in" the Absolute is therefore not to be understood primarily in a spatial manner:

> Of course, in our vernacular, all words that describe relations between things are taken in the first instance from space, such as: "in", "outside", "on", "over", "under", "next to", "out". Or, rather, in ordinary pre-scientific consciousness they are mostly understood only from space. But all these words must be spiritualized (*vergeistigt*) and taken in a super-sensory way (*auf übersinnliche Weise*) if they are used consistently with philosophical Science. It is therefore not permissible for the philosopher to distort (*verdrehen*) these words, as if he were speaking of spatial relations, even when he helps himself uses these words to designate the relation between the finite and the infinite. (Krause 1869: 308).

For God's relationship to the world, this understanding of the world's being in God, according to Krause, follows:

> Through this, therefore, is proven the fundamentally important distinction between the following two propositions: *The world is outside of God*, and *The world is outside of God as the Ur-Essence*. The first sentence is fundamentally false, because apart from [Or-Essence] nothing is conceivable, in that the infinity and unconditionality of God would be denied by the slightest external appearance. But the other sentence: that the world is outside of and under God, insofar as God is *Ur-Essence*, states a fundamental essential property of God (*eine Grundwesenheit Gottes*). (Krause 1828: 310)

That is:

> I distinguish God from the world, as prior to, and over and above the world, that is, as Ur-Essence, God as Ur-Essence is demarcated, distinguished, from the whole world (*abgegrenzt unterschieden von der ganzen Welt*). Therefore, the world is thought outside of, and under God as Ur-Essence. (Krause 1828: 310)

In more detail, based on the distinction between Or-Essence and Ur-Essence, Krause is able to infer:

> Therefore, the old dispute about the relation of God to the world, "whether God is extra-worldly, and the world is an extra-divine being, or not," is satisfactorily solved. For, by distinguishing [the Absolute] from itself as Ur-Essence, it is seen that God, as one, is the self-same whole Or-Essence, neither outside nor above, nor on, nor in the world. But, certainly, in Himself, under Himself, and through Himself, God is also the world (*auch die Welt ist*). Also, God as Ur-Essence is outside and above the world. And the world is outside of Him as Ur-Essence. And, finally, God as Ur-Essence is also united with the world, united with Reason, with Nature, and with the union of both, as also with humanity (Krause 1828: 401).

This dialectic of relations between the finite and conditioned, and the infinite and unconditioned, in Krause's panentheism is derived from his metaphysical mereology. As the one, self-same and whole being, as *Or-Essence*, the Absolute is in and through itself the world. As a whole, which has metaphysical priority over its parts, as the ground of the unity of its essence, as *Ur-Essence*, the world is outside of the Absolute. In Krause's system, therefore, the Absolute does not have to first mediate dialectically with itself, as in Hegel, but is recognized as something that has always already been differentiated and mediated in itself.

To illustrate his metaphysical mereology, Krause developed the following diagram. It not only clarifies the structure of the Absolute and its relationship to the world but may also be read as a fundamental mereological scheme of the possible relations between a whole and its parts, as well as their relations:

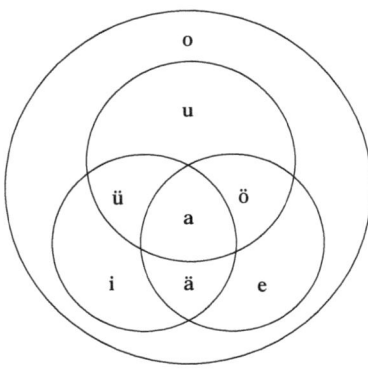

While "o" designates the one, self-same and whole Absolute as *Or-Essence*, outside of which nothing is, nor is conceivable, "u" designates the Absolute as *Ur-Essence*, in virtue of having logical priority over its parts. And it includes Independence ("i") as well as Wholeness ("e"), also in their union ("ä"), and may be viewed as its constitutive ground. "ü," "a" and "ö" designate the relations of the parts as particular or combined parts of the whole of which they are parts.

4. Krause's Cosmopolitanism

If the Absolute as *Or-Essence* is not opposed to the world, but the world is a relational-intrinsic determination of the Absolute, and if the Absolute is everything finite in itself as a (metaphysical) part, then it follows, according to Krause, that the spatio-temporal history of the world is an intrinsic-relational determination of the Absolute as well. What happens in the world is not without consequences for the Absolute, because the history of the world is metaphysically nothing other than the one life of the Absolute; everything that happens in the world is part of the one divine life, because in *sensu stricto* only the Absolute exists:

> God is in Himself the one life, supremely as Ur-Essence, but then as being in Himself the organism of all final-beings or finite beings (*Endwesen oder endlichen Wesen*). Therefore, the one life of God contains the life of Reason, the life of Nature, and both united as the life of Humanity. (Krause 1874: 188)

Because, furthermore, according to Krause, the Absolute as the one self-same and whole Being is the free cause of its infinite life; it follows that every free finite being *ipso facto* participates in the infinite freedom of the Absolute. As Krause says:

> God freely causes the steady becoming of His one life, and, like Him, all finite beings also cause their inner finite life in Him with finite freedom. [...] The one life of God is an organic whole. And all finite beings, insofar as they live, are also united with each other, and with God as the Ur-Essence. And every finite life of every finite being is a finite organic whole, akin to the one organic life of God, therefore also the life of every human being and the life of humanity. (Krause 1874: 188)[27]

For Krause, humanity encompasses all people, including not only the living, but also past and future generations of humankind, because "all people in all times and countries, from Adam onwards, belong to the one great whole of humankind" (Krause 1900: 4). Therefore:

> Under "humanity" [...] is always understood the whole one unity-of-essence (*Eine Vereinwesen*) of Reason and Nature in Essence (*Wesen*), that is, in God.

---

27 See also Krause (1820: iii). "The idea of the one whole, of the unity and harmonious organization of all its parts in, with and through each other and through the whole, is ever more clearly recognized, ever more purely loved, and always, as the primal idea of God, the world and humankind raised to the law of all human activity.—Humankind itself and its life is more and more considered as an organic whole, and all human things are formed as subordinate parts of this whole, in harmony among themselves and with the whole."

> This is both the universally human, and the epitome of all individual human beings, united in a single whole life (*in Einem Lebenganzen*). (Krause 1820: lxxvii, fn)

On Krause's panentheism, the freedom of each human individual, consequently, is nothing but a finite part of God's absolute freedom, who is every finite being in Himself:

> The freedom that I have is God's; a primal (*urendlicher*), inner part of the one freedom of the Absolute (*der Einen Freiheit Wesens*). For I am not an independent being (*alleinständiges Wesen*), but the Absolute in itself is me (*Wesen ist in sich ich*). [...] This [freedom] is an originally finite (*urendliche*) freedom that God has 'allowed (lent)' ('*gelassen (verliehen)*') to himself, [as being in himself the world]. (Krause 1892b: 125)

If human beings are free, however, it follows that the historical development of humanity is free as well, where Krause understands freedom not as freedom of indifference, but as freedom for excellence.

> It is the only task of life, the purely spiritual, the purely physical, and the human: to form [...] the general and the eternal [...] in the finite, individual and temporal. (Krause 1811a number 27: 110)

Consequently, Krause's panentheism, which is initially developed from the phenomenological self-observation of the Ego, and then identifies the world as a relational-intrinsic determination of the Absolute, leads to the need to specify, in a philosophical social theory, how each human being and humanity as a whole *ought* to use its freedom.

4.1 Social Theory, Cosmopolitanism, and the Concept of the Human League

For Krause, philosophical social theory is the "science of ideas and laws according to which independent, free rational beings (*freie Vernunftwesen*) unite in a good and beautiful life so that they live like one rational being" (Krause 1868: VIII footnote). The goal of social theory is to show how a society should be organized, so that the ideal of humanity—the Human Archetype—may be regarded as realized in it.

According to Krause, to achieve this goal, there are three tasks a social theory has to fulfill: A social theory has to (a) specify the ideal of humanity (*Urbild der Menschheit*), (b) to gather information about the current social conditions and their historical development, and (c) to develop a political agenda how to change the current social conditions in order to realize the archetype of human society. The ideal of humanity—the *Urbild der Menschheit*—must first be recognized, since it is both the *archetype* and the *teleotype* of humankind:

> The archetypes represent what really *should* be lived. And by means of them, those conceptual images (*Begriffbilder*) come about that refer to the model concept (*Musterbegriff*) of something-to-be-realized (*eines Zu-Verwirklichenden*) in accordance with the idea. They may therefore be called 'model images' (*Musterbilder*). (Krause 1836: 336)
>
> The knowledge of history, of the concept of history, and of the inherent model concept (*eigenleblichen Musterbegriffes*) and model image (*Musterbildes*) of the Human League may only be gained as an inner part of the similar knowledge of the entire nascent life of this terrestrial humanity. [...] Only in this totality of historical-scientific knowledge is it even possible to discover and appreciate the historical beginnings of the Human League on this Earth, and to recognize both what can and should be done for the education of the Human League, now and in every future. (Krause 1820: cv)[28]

In general, based on the proper understanding of the Human Archetype, a historically informed view of the current state of the art, according to Krause, has to recognize discrepancies between the archetype and the current historical conditions and, because of this, political agendas must be worked out, for how the Human Archetype may be more completely realized in the historical here and now. This assessment of the form and task of social theory, which brings Krause close to critical theory, has lost none of its relevance for current discussions.

4.1.1 The Human League

The central concept of Krause's social theory is the concept of the Human League (*Menschheitbund*). According to Krause, the concept of the Human League was developed in the years 1807/1808 and may be understood as expressing the central idea of his social theory. Krause (1891: 225) describes the predecessors of the idea of the Human League as follows:

> The ancestral experiments of the Human League have always emanated from scientists and goddesses inspired by Science. So: Pythagoras, Plato, Essener, Jesus, Culdeer, Val. Andrea, Jordanus Bruno, Comenius, Leibniz (see his *Inedita*), Desaguliers, Anderson, Herder (who knew both writings exactly), Fessler.

---

28 Cf. López-Morrillas (1981: 38): "Humankind, says Krause, shows signs of turning away from its age-old alienation and is beginning to bend its steps toward universal solidarity, based on rational realization of the common dependence of all men and their subordination to God and divine laws. Placed in this context, the word *Urbild* acquires a dual meaning. On the one hand it means *archetype*, an original pattern; but on the other it has the same meaning as *teleotype*, the final form to be assumed by human solidarity." See also Vester (1993: 26) and Ahrens (1871: 266 ff.).

However, Krause claimed originality for the idea of the Human League, which he conceived and made concrete:

> The idea of the Human League was first proclaimed by me, as an intrinsic result of my Scientific System. And I had no inkling or knowledge of this idea either from oral or from written communication, borrowed neither from an open nor from a secret society. (Krause 1843: 472)[29]

Although Krause attempted various clarifications of the concept of the Human League in the course of his work, the core idea did not vary. For Krause, "The Human League" is always the name of the ideal state of the global civil society that is to be historically realized by humanity and therefore designates

> the essential, artful society of all people on earth, in which they unite as people to be as one, a whole and organic humanity (*um als Eine, eine ganze und organische Menschheit zu sein*), to live and grow in themselves and in all their relationships to God, to Nature and to Reason, and to humanity in the universe (Weltall). (Krause 1900: 1)

The Human League, accordingly, is:

> The social union of all human beings as pure, whole, human beings for the whole life of humankind. The Human League, as the league for the whole, pure, human life, is by its essence (nature) a league that encompasses all people. Not only can and should all people participate, but, before this is the case, they themselves do not live up to their idea. Only then is it a league for everything human. It engages the members of all other societies without disturbing the connections which they have, as members of other societies. It thereby becomes the most secure and most irrepressible force (*Gewalt*) on earth. In it, the quiet, peaceful harmony of all human things and societies, among themselves, is formed and maintained, simply through the power of reason and feeling, through the gentle means of love. (Krauses 1900: 426)

As an all-encompassing civil society, the Human League is not only the ideal of social coexistence, but, metaphysically, an image of the inner organism of the Absolute:

> The Human League [is] not a society alongside, or just a society 'outside-above' (*ausserüber*), the state, church, and Masonic Brotherhood. But, as Essence (*Wesen*) is related to the structure of Essence (*Wesengliedbau*), as its inner Essence (*Inwesenthume*), so the Human League is related to human society as a

---

29 For a more thoroughgoing analysis of the influence of Freemasonry on Krause's thinking, which, contrary to Krause's statements, was probably greater than he admitted in later years, see Horn (1985).

whole. Therefore, the Human League has all other human societies in-under itself (*inunter sich*). (Krause 1890: 124)³⁰

4.1.2 The Equal Value of All Human Beings

The concept of the Human League, according to Krause, implies the equal value of all people, regardless of their origin, gender, or physical constitution. The equality and dignity of all people results solely from their *Godlikeness*, which is grounded in and through the panentheistically understood Absolute.³¹ As Dierksmeier (2016a: 139) states:

> According to Krause, however, one may neither obtain nor forfeit the recognition of human dignity. The fundamental right of all human beings to be recognized as moral rational beings is, therefore, not based on reciprocity of factual recognition, which is always conditional. Rather, the unconditional right to be respected as a rational being establishes an absolute legal obligation for universal recognition.

Krause is therefore able to state that

> all people are equal (*gleich*). They are next to each other, not among each other. No one is subject to the other. But, all together, they obey the law of God in moral freedom (*dem Gesetze Gottes in sittlicher Freiheit*). (Krause 1890: 127)³²

For Krause, it was therefore obvious that there is absolute equality of man and woman, too. As Krause puts it:

> Man and woman are equally essential to humanity, so woman is in no way subordinate to man. In all her powers of spirit and heart and body, woman is just as capable and original as man in all parts of human destiny. (Krause 2022: 102)³³

---

30 See also Dierksmeier (1999: 79): "Humankind is drawn together by Krause across the boundaries of living space and historical time into one subject. Humankind is conceived as a full (*vollwertiges*) legal subject (*Rechtssubjekt*), because it is self-referential (*selbstbezügliches*). For every action (*Handlung*) that takes place within it has (potentially) a retro-active effect on the whole of humanity."

31 Because, for Krause, the right to a dignified life follows from the metaphysically determined essence of the human being, Krause would agree with Rödl (2017: 36) that: "[the] price of renouncing a natural law foundation for human rights […] is evident in their degradation to a question of taste."

32 Cf. also Krumpel (1990: 159) and Rabe (2006a: 155), Rabe (2006).

33 See also Dierksmeier (1999: 77): "Krause's legal-philosophical writings, which have not gone unnoticed, always end with demands that sound incredibly modern. So Krause speaks completely against the trend of his time, about the unrestricted equality of women, the equality of races, the intrinsic value of children, the rights of Nature and even something like intergenerational justice, embryo protection, and the rights of the deceased. Krause knows about intellectual rights (*geistige Rechte*) and rights to intellectual works. He addresses

Because of the equal value of man and woman, Krause vehemently opposes the oppression of women by men:

> The female sex is just as capable of all-round, particular and consistent development as the male. And humanity itself remains only imperfectly and partially educated as long as the beautiful, weaker sex of women, ungratefully and unfeelingly oppressed by the brute strength of men, has to lag behind the male in some part of human determination. Virtue and love, science and art, law and religion, all must first be shaped and perfected in a male and female way before humankind can boast of having expressed itself harmoniously on all sides. The triumph of humankind is only male and female uniform education, in free harmonious interplay. (Krause 2022: 103)

Furthermore:

> In contradiction to all spiritual and physical and human experience and history, one has wanted to claim that the woman is spiritually and physically on a lower level of education, that the women are only unfinished men [...]. Likewise, the assertion that the entire destiny of woman is exhausted in her relationship as a mother and that the female half of humanity is not destined to participate in public social life is contrary to nature and the destiny of man. The sexual function and the moral and legal consequences of it (education of children, household) do not cancel out, either for man or for woman, the demand and the possibility of general human education and of a predominant life profession (in all parts of human destiny). And as far as especially the procreation, care and education of the children are concerned, both sexes have an equally essential, equally necessary and, as already the similarity of the children shows, equally intimate share and thus as rational beings equally justified obligation. (Krause 1882d: 272f.)

4.1.3 The Human League and Cosmopolitism

Cosmopolitanism, according to Krause, describes the ideal state of global civil society in which

> every human being and every human society exists in, through and with (*in, durch und mit*) the whole, in and for itself (*in und für sich selbst*) and essentially lives (*wesenlebet*). And all only determine each other, liberate each other, guide each other, educate each other and strengthen each other for the good (*und sich alle nur zum Guten wechselbestimmen, wechselbefreien, wechselanleiten, wechselbilden und wechselbekräftigen*). (Krause 1873: 14)

In more detail:

> Q: But what is the main internal work and overall work of the Human League?
> A: The independent and social (absolute and synthetic, or harmonious)

---

issues of social distributive justice, and discusses problems of supra-national legal systems." For the role of women in Krause, and its historical record, see also Wollgast (2016: 244 ff.) and Rabe (2006).

purification, ennoblement, and new formation and completion (full development) of all subordinate societies in humanity, in accordance with the idea (the ought concept (*Sollbegriffe*)) as a complete, all-over-coherent (*allübereinstimmigen*), healthy, powerful and beautiful organism. In this way, every human being, and every human society, exists and essentially lives (*wesenlebet*) in, through, and with, the whole, in and for itself. And all only determine themselves through change, free themselves through change, guide themselves by change, educate themselves by change, and reinforce each other through change, only for the Good (*und sich alle nur zum Guten wechselbestimmen, wechselbefreien, wechselanleiten, wechselbilden und wechselbekräftigen*). So, finally, all essential-selves (persons) (*Selbwesen (Personen)*) in humanity are mature as in one essential-self (*als in Einem Selbwesen*), so that no one patronizes the other. But each one is connected with everyone, and everyone with each one, in God-like freedom, to present the one Good as the everything-like (*allartigen*) Good, to the presentation of the one, same, whole, God-like and God-unified essential life (*gottvereinten Wesenlebens*) of humankind. (Krause 1873: 14)

Against this background, Krause's concept of the Human League is nothing but a political cosmopolitanism that follows from a moral cosmopolitanism, which in turn is based on Krause's panentheism. As Krause says:

> Considering the relation of human being to human being, to the world and to God, shows up the noticable appearance of cosmopolitanism (*Weltbürgerthums*) and humanity (*Menschheitthumes*) or cosmopolitanism (*Kosmopolitismus*) and philanthropism (*Philanthropismus*). [...] It is now also possible to regard the human being, whose own idea has also already been recognized, as a member and comrade of the humanity of this place of residence, this celestial body, indeed the whole universe. And when this thought is taken up into feeling, and also placed in relation to the will, then the attitude arises, which one designates with the name "world citizenship" or "cosmopolitanism," or, the attitude that every human being as a human being is a member and citizen of the cosmos, of the universe, according to the eternal truth, prior to and over and above all historical statutes, and independently of them, and to treat every human being in this way and to live with them in this sense. If attention is now paid to the fact that every human being is first and foremost a member of this humanity, and should therefore be respected, loved, lived with, and treated as such, then, from this, further arises the sense of humanity peculiar to this period, philanthropism. This is the intimacy with humanity as purely human, or the human attitude which recognizes in every human being a member of humanity who is fundamentally equal to all other human beings, having equal authority and dignity. Now this threefold attitude, and the threefold striving based on it, that of theism, cosmopolitanism and philanthropism, are in themselves purely good, purely essential, and they signify, and make possible, essential advances on the path of humankind to the fulfillment of its life. (Krause 1843: 358–359)[34]

---

34 For an analysis of cosmopolitan ideas around 1800, see Albrecht (2005). See also Cavallar (2003: 182): "Krause is a cosmopolitan who thinks in global

4.2 The Structure of the Human League

The parts of the Human League, which Krause also calls 'leagues' (*Bünde*), are social units and social communities. These are, based on the degree of existential involvement of the constituent members and based on their purpose, divided into fundamental societies (*Grundgesellschaften*), laboring societies (*werktätige Gesellschaften*), and self-laboring societies (*selbstwerktätige Gesellschaften*):

> Human sociability first marries the whole individuals for their own sake. Or, it unites only a part of their life for the production and display of definite social works. I will call the first societies 'fundamental-societies' (*Grundgesellschaften*), but the others 'laboring-societies' (*werktätige Gesellschaften*). But, humanity is, at one and the same time, its own master and its own work (*Werk*). Humanity makes itself, and its whole individuality, the object of its own social endeavor as well. Humanity founds societies for nurture and mutual education. These societies, in which Humankind rejuvenates and educates itself socially, I will call 'self-working' unions (*selbstwerkthätige*). (Krause 2022: 97–98)

While fundamental societies always affect the whole person, there is a specific purpose for laboring societies that is to be realized in and through them. The self-laboring societies are those whose purpose is the educational self-forming of the people involved.[35]

With the distinction between fundamental societies, work societies and self-work societies, Krause has grasped, in principle, all fundamental societal forms of a functionally differentiated society, which is to say that this distinction may be used to identify any social unit of the Human League as a fundamental society, work-society or self-laboring-society:

> [Through the distinction between fundamental-societies, work-societies and self-laboring-societies] a natural order (*naturgemäße Ordnung*) results which, without ever losing sight of the whole of humanity and its sociability, *we may*

---

dimensions. His political cosmopolitanism is based on natural law, which leads to the idea of a global legal league (*globalen Rechtsbundes*)."

35 See Dierksmeier (2003a: 399): "Because [for Krause] general-human and individual-specific self-realization is impossible without a minimum of education, the result is a right of the general public to that essential education. Krause declares it to be the task of a separate educational art to empower people through autonomous guidance (education) for self-education (education) (*durch autonomes Lenken (Erziehung) zur Selbsterziehung (Bildung)*) and self-sufficient control of themselves. General-human and individual-specific educational conditions must be balanced with each other, in such a way that the intellectual differences of those to be educated are indeed taken into account, but an axiological difference between them is not opened."

certainly consider as all individual societies both in their independence and in their all-round social harmony. (Krause 2022: 98, emphasis BPG)[36]

4.2.1 The Fundamental Societies: Marriage, Friendship, and Free Socializing

In order to spell out the functionally differentiated structure of the Human League as a global civil society designed according to the idea of humanity, Krause starts with the individual human being and distinguishes three basic forms of fundamental societies that people may freely enter into with other people: (a) marriage, (b) friendship, and (c) free socializing.

(a) Marriage, for Krause, is a union of man and woman based on free love that not only embraces the whole human being as the individual that they are but is also involved as the nucleus of the rejuvenation of society due to its openness to procreation. As Krause (2022: 138–139) states: "All this is, viewed divinely in itself, one act (*an sich, auf göttliche Weise betrachtet, Ein Act*): the creation of new people, the constant rejuvenation and the regulated growth of the human race on Earth, the protection and upbringing of children, and the loving co-existence of parents and children in uninterrupted, increasingly higher personality." Marriage, according to Krause, thus implies the absolute equality of man and woman, even if man and woman are not the same. Because the reason for marriage is the love between man and woman, marriage as a fundamental society exists just so long as marital love between man and woman exists: "Love in general does not want to enforce, for as soon as it wanted to enforce, it would destroy itself, thus causing the other party to step out of the marriage. The marriage contract is not a contract of submission, on the part of neither the woman nor the man" (Krause 1803: 197–198). When love has expired, then the man or the woman is free to end the marriage. As Krause (1900: 108) says: "Married couples may separate as they wish, but in a legal, humane, way and with similar ceremonies to those with which the marriage was made. Enforced marriage is often worse than enforced work in the galley!"[37]

---

36 See Gil (1988: 104). "Krause develops [...] a metaphysically grounded theory of socialization which, due to its complexity and its theoretical level of sophistication, is categorically able to do justice to all interpretation mechanisms, subsystems, contexts, fields, and 'work federations' that condition human action and are conditioned by it."

37 Krause's sexual ethics were surprisingly modern because, for Krause, it is ultimately within the freedom of the individual, whom they enter into a sexual relationship with: "I see nothing contrary to humanity and God when two, yes

(b) Besides marriage, the second type of fundamental society is friendship. While marriage is based on free love and the desire for offspring, the ground of friendship is the different and harmoniously complementary individuality of the people involved, beyond the sex drive, being conducive to this independent fundamental society. Because "close friends [become] like one heart and one soul" (Krause 2022: 122), friendship as a social institution is for Krause, along with marriage, a *conditio sine qua non* for the establishment of the Human League: Without friendship "neither individual human beings nor social associations could be formed in their reciprocity. Nor could the whole wealth of human characters be developed as an organic whole" (Krause 2022: 121). Although friendship is primarily a relationship between individuals, for Krause it is not limited to the area of the individual, but may exist between random social units: "The various systems of friendship wind freely through families, and all other social associations. And friends are recognized by the state, by the church, and by laboring-societies, as higher persons (*als höhere Personen*), and as such are incorporated into their interior (*in ihr Inneres aufgenommen*)" (Krause 2022: 127).

(c) Finally, the free sociability of the human being consists in the fact that people gather together for the realization of a specific purpose, independently of marriage and friendship with other people. This purpose can either be intrinsic aesthetic entertainment and free play or the extrinsic realization of a specific goal.

The social bonds constituted by marriage, friendship and free sociability do not stand unrelated to one another within the Human League. Rather, they are always already related to one another, in the sense of a functionally differentiated and harmonious society, and they condition and promote one another:

> These three fundamental human societies thrive only when they live as an organic whole in, with, and through each other. Within the family there is friendship and free conviviality. Free company cheers and enlivens friendship. In free sociability (*in freier Geselligkeit*), people who are made to be friends and spouses recognize each other. (Krause 2022: 134)

---

several couples, who are all friends, also love each other physically. Every man joins with each of the connected women, and also every woman copulates with each of the associated men, also socially. Life-scorching lust and sexual outrage would, of course, certainly not be kindled in people who are purely godly and united in social love between the sexes, even in rougher conditions. A marriage between two must have its own bliss, if pure and beautiful in a heartfelt way" (Krause 1900: 203).

Marriage, friendship and free sociability, according to Krause, are the three fundamental societies that an individual may enter into. They constitute the fundamental societies of the first order, "which unite individuals as individuals in a way conducive to life (*lebendig*) by marrying the basic opposites of gender, character, and individuality in life (*im Leben*)" (Krause 2022: 135).[38] Every human society of a higher order results as a combination of the fundamental societies of marriage, friendship and free sociability in the league of humankind, until finally the highest society, the Human League on earth, is reached.[39]

Krause formulates the principle behind the constitution of the different higher-order unions as follows:

> Each yet higher union (*Verein*) of individuals may be essentially recognized by the fact that several truly opposed (*entgegengesetzte*) individuals of the next lower association really live together in a common higher area as one human being (*als Ein Mensch zusammen leben*). (Krause 2022: 135).

That is:

> A next-higher (*Nebenhöheres*) is a higher, sociable whole, which consists of nothing but next-beings (*Nebenwesen*). [...] So marriages, local communities, tribes, peoples, part-humanities of a star (*Theilmenschheiten eines Sternes*), are a series of next-highers. The union (*ens collectivum*) of next-beings becomes something higher, only through the organic character of society, through the distribution of functions and processes to special, self-sufficient organs (*selbheitliche Organe*). (Krause 1890: 73 FN)

The higher fundamental societies, the higher "persons" in humanity, include: the family association as a union of different families, the tribe as a union of different family associations, the people's association as a union of different tribes, and, finally, terrestrial humanity as a peaceful union of all people's associations on earth.[40] For Krause, each of these fundamental societies is an independent social unit that is constituted on the basis of

---

38 See Dierksmeier (2016a: 169): "In Krause's thinking, the group of persons (*Personenverbund*) is not artificially added to individual existence (*Individualexistenz*). Rather, it presents there a natural form of the human realization of freedom (*Freiheitsverwirklichung*)."

39 Krause assumed that there is human life on other planets, and that the highest fundamental society is the humanity populating the universe. If there is rational, extraterrestrial life, then Krause would also count these life forms as part of the Human League. For the unity of persons consists in their being physical rational beings.

40 Cf. Krause (1820: lxxxiii): "By the expression: 'inner selfhood of humankind' (*innere Selbwesen der Menschheit*) I understand the otherwise so-called moral persons in humankind. These are, in ascending order: the individual, marriage,

the voluntary social cooperation of the people gathered in it.[41] And, as the realization of the idea of humanity, each is entitled to goods to be provided by global civil society, in order to be able to realize its purpose. For example, the family needs a house and garden in order to be able to lead a decent life. Friendship and free sociability need public spaces, to be able to gather. And people need a territory on which they can live, according to their own cultural characteristics.[42]

Based on Krause's combinatorial view of social fundamental societies that constitute the Human League, the following scheme of the structure of the fundamental "persons" in the Human League results:

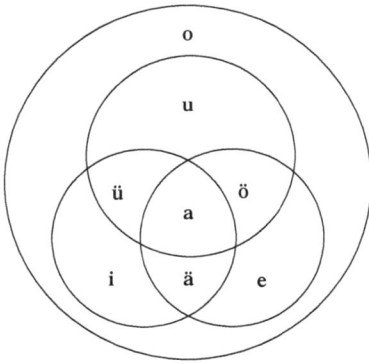

The fundamental societies of the first order are constituted by marriage, friendship, and free sociability, by the single individuals—i, e and u. Based on this, the fundamental societies of a higher order are formed by combinatorial iteration: For example, if i, e and u are families, o as a family

---

friendship, freedom of society, tribe, people, people's association, earthly humanity, right up to the one humanity in God."

41 Cf. Krause (1893: 11): "A federation of states (*Staatenbund*) is: several states, just in case they have legally combined to establish the law amongst themselves as higher persons (entire peoples) in a social way. All peoples united for this purpose are thereby free, internally and externally. Their lives are able to develop more and more perfectly; morally free according to the development of the laws peculiar to each people."

42 See also Dierksmeier (2016a: 172–173): "Two things stand out for today's consideration: Krause emphasizes that voluntary integration into collectives is important as an expression of individual freedom. It distinguishes it from atomistic liberalisms. On the other hand, because he also sees freedom as the ground of the validity (*Geltungsgrund*) of those ties, he also differs from positions that were dubbed 'romantic' at the time, and now 'communitarian.'"

association is a fundamental society of a higher order. If i, e, and u are peoples, o makes a League of Nations, etc.

Because the individual fundamental societies in the Human League have a certain autonomy, as an expression of human social freedom, it follows that the Human League has a *subsidiary structure*: Every social sphere at every level of the social order should, as far as possible, look after its own interests; regulate and realize the ideal of humanity in their own way.[43] This is because every social unit "is destined to fulfill the entire human destiny in its own way" (Krause 1820: lxxxxv). Beyond the provision of the necessary goods, the Human League, thereby "allows all individual institutes to improve their inner deficiencies of their own accord and according to their own laws" (Krause 1820: viii).[44]

4.2.2 The Laboring Societies for the Fundamental Forms of Life

To realize the ideal of humanity beyond the fundamental societies, the people in the Human League unite in laboring societies. These Krause divides into (a) laboring societies for the fundamental forms of life and (b) those for the fundamental works of life.[45]

The purpose of the laboring societies for the fundamental forms of life is that the people in them shape their social conditions in the sense of global governance according to the ideals of (a) *virtue*, (b) *law*, (c) *beauty*, and (d) *godliness*.[46]

---

43 In the current debate, Krause would agree with Benhabib (2016: 82): "Furthermore, as 'concrete' and 'generalized' others, human beings are beings who are embodied and vulnerable, and therefore dependent on the care and solidarity of others. Such people are only capable of freedom and autonomy through social upbringing and education."
44 See also Vester (1933: 11): "It is particularly important to emphasize that each individual level has its own life, the '*vita propria*'. Their relative independence, freedom, and autonomy, are preserved. And it is not absorbed in the subsequent higher level. Rather, the lower level is the fundamental condition, the carrier and the immediate source of life for the higher level."
45 See also Krause (1900: 7–8) for an overview of the structure of the Human League, which also includes the individual professions.
46 Cf. Conradi (1938: 70): "The solution of the practical tasks of life requires the coalition (*Zusammenschluß*) of citizens in estates, leagues and unions in order to realize certain rational goals with collective strength. Krause lists several unions of this kind: unions for art, science, law, education, agriculture, industry, trade and the 'unions for useful art', the trades. The rights to which these unions are entitled are determined according to their respective purpose, and their relationship to the other unions."

(a) Because "virtue [...] is the artistic doing and free-will accomplishment of pure goodness in a godlike life" (Krause 1900: 473), the aim of the league of virtue (*Tugendbund*) as a laboring society for the fundamental forms of life is to enable every individual to lead a virtuous life: "The Virtue Covenant is essential to humankind's perfection. Humankind establishes the unity, harmony, strength, and beauty (*Einheit, Harmonie, Stärke und Schönheit*) of all human powers. Only where it is closed on earth does a truly human life of virtue begin. [The Virtue Covenant] strengthens humankind so that it completes its whole life beautifully in clear self-confidence. In [the Virtue Covenant] the individual moral human also finds the external condition of his own moral life. Then the hindrances to virtue, the incentives to vice, which the individual encounters in his higher moral striving in the still imperfect society, have disappeared. Public moral life (*das öffentliche sittliche Leben*) is the model and the nourishment of his particular moral development (*eigenthümlichen sittlichen Ausbildung*)" (Krause 2022: 216).

(b) The league of virtue is intended to enable all people to achieve the good out of moral freedom. In contrast, the league of right does not require that the good be done out of a specific inner attitude. It regulates external social coexistence at all levels independently of the moral intention of the individual. As Krause (2022: 291–292) states: "As we have seen, the individual person should be just as active in establishing the law as every family and every tribe, even as every laboring-society of people. Each in its own sphere, each free and independent, but also in this striving, all should be united socially and be subordinate to the higher personal whole, ultimately to humankind itself." The specific goal of the league of right is to implement a legal order applicable to the *global governance* of humankind by a cosmopolitan society. This goes hand in hand with a distribution of goods that formally and materially enables every human society to realize its individual essence in freedom. As Krause (1811a: number 27. 107) argues: "The archetype of law (*Urbild des Rechtes*) demands that: On, and in, every being (*Wesen*) everything is realised that is necessary for all other beings to be perfected; independently, and socially in their living conditions. For example, in order to make the legal relationship clearer: If there are several beings a, b, c, d, ... in a higher collective, on a common area in a living community, then the law demands that a in their acts and omissions, and suffering, is so determined that also, b, c, d ..., are and become, all that they are destined to be and to become (*Alles das seyen und werden, was zu seyn und zu werden sie bestimmt sind*). The same applies to those in connection, ab, ac, ad, ..., bc, bd, ..., cd ...

and abc, abd, bcd, ... so long as, and in so far as, they are connected with *a* in life. And the same is also required of b, c, d ..., of ab, ac, ad ... bc, bd, ... Abc, abd ... abcd ..." In other words, "the law is the elemental structure of the condition of the life of a being, which depends on free will: Every rational being is provided with the totality of conditions for the achievement of its destiny (*Bestimmung*). In virtue of this, every rational being, from their side, provides all other rational beings with the conditions for the attainment of their destiny, insofar as such beings depend on their freedom" (Krause 1900: 474). The law therefore should not only enable every being to realize their own idea in time, but also to live in such a way that their life respects the same unconditional right of all other legal subjects to a life in accordance with their essence. For Krause, legal empowerment must be strictly distinguished from legal coercion. In Krause's system, the league of right does not lead to a night-watchman state that obliges people to live a certain life. But rather, in the spirit of the *ius cosmopoliticum*, it only creates the legal conditions that ensure a decent life *enabled* in and by freedom. As Krause (1811a: 14, number 4) states: "The law is therefore the archetypal form of all beings, according to which each one is determined in its entire life by the idea of every other, with which it lives together, and ultimately by the idea of all beings living together in God."[47] Understood in this way, "Right [...] [requires], affirmatively, a certain quality of all things (*bestimmte Beschaffenheit aller Dinge*)" (Krause 1811a number 7: 26). These are requirements implied by the metaphysical essence of legal subjects. Therefore, legal positivism is excluded in Krause's system: "The essence of Right (*Wesen des Rechtes*) does not rest in the arbitrariness of humankind, of individuals, or of any being, but rather in the unchanging essence of God, in the Nature of things, and in the laws of life (*Gesetzen des Lebens*)" (Krause 2022: 224). Instead, for Krause, there is a right to law that is metaphysically based on human essence, a right which can be called a right to the right or "a right for the sake of the right"

---

47 See Dierksmeier (2016a: 157): "Legal freedom protects the potential of rational freedom: Moral freedom (*sittliche Freiheit*) realizes it. The freedom that is to be legally protected should enable the moral self-orientation of individuals, not force it." See also Krumpel (1990: 158): "The state is not the reality of the moral idea (Hegel), but only a legal institution. It has no overriding juristiction (*Obervormundschaft*) over the totality of human affairs. The merely formal individualistic liberalism, which presented the state as the overarching concept of political power, should be replaced by a conception of participatory democracy, self-regulation and political openness."

(Krause 1843: 205 FN): For every human being has a pre-legal entitlement to the essential conditions of his or her life being fulfilled. But, by this, Krause anticipates a thought which is later found in Hannah Arendt. Arendt (1995: 465) argues "that the right to rights (*das Recht auf Rechte*), or the right of every human being to belong to humankind, must be guaranteed by humankind itself."[48]

(c) People gather in the virtue-league and the law-league to establish the conditions of inner and outer freedom for humankind. But the league of divinity (*Gottinnigkeitbund*) focuses on cultivating the religious mind of the people. Krause primarily identifies the love for God as that which is appropriate to the religious mind, in order to base the love for all finite beings on this love for God in the sense of his panentheism. For they are all parts of the Absolute: "The truly devout (*weseninnige*) human being recognizes and loves all things in every single aspect of their life, as members of the one *ur-essence* and *ur-life* (*als Glieder des Einen Urwesens und Urlebens*). Their open mind is just as devoutly directed to the eternal as to individual life; just as much to what remains in all time as to what is eternally revealed in time. They recognize and love everything, as a being in God (*als ein Wesen in Gott*), and live with everything as a being subsidiary to God (*als mit einem Nebenwesen in Gott*). All devotion of man and humankind is devotion to God, because [309] all that is, is in God, and only God is (*Alles was ist, in Gott ist, und weil nur Gott ist*)" (Krause 2022: 235). Therefore: "It is impossible to truly love God without lovingly embracing all things. And so every loving being is filled with one love, with love for God, and, for all beings, in Him" (Krause 2022: 86). For Krause, against this background, the purpose of the League of Divinity consists in awakening in all people the all-encompassing love for God and for everything finite. This is in order to enable them to live a holistic life that goes beyond the intellectual vision of the Absolute, in which the theoretically viewed agrees consistently with the emotional life of people.

(d) Finally, the League of Beauty is based on the knowledge that God is the "original source of all beauty (*Urquelle aller Schönheit*)" (Krause 2022: 52). Therefore, "the first task of the League of Beauty is continually ongoing social research into the knowledge of beauty, its eternal

---

48 See Arendt (1991) and (1949). See also Reinhardt (2021: 247–248): "Arendt therefore proposes that civil and human rights should be supplemented with a "right to rights" (*Recht auf Rechte*): the right to be a member of a legal community (*Rechtsgemeinschaft*), because only by belonging to a legal community could human rights also be protected."

idea, and its living individual appearance in the life of all beings, in the whole life of the Earth, but especially in the life of humankind" (Krause 2022: 247). Because everything finite is in God, it also participates in God's beauty: "God is well-pleased to see himself in the beauty of creatures, and the creatures as worthy of him. In beauty, the world proves itself to be the work of the eternal Master" (Krause 2022: 52). The aim of the league of beauty is to promote the knowledge of beauty. This is in order to shape social life in accordance with the ideal of beauty, based on this knowledge: "This independent association [...] has the purpose of making all human life accord purely to the archetype of beauty (*den Urbilde der Schönheit*), to be fulfilled as a beautiful work of art" (Krause 2022: 247). In other words: "As with all societies, the main business of its assemblies (*Versammlungen*) is to awaken individuals, so that they lead their lives according to the model of beauty. Therefore, the whole League has to watch that the whole of human life; the National League, Tribe League, Family League and Friend's League for Beauty, are such that the national life, the tribal life, the family and friends life are clothed in particular beauty. The Beauty League, as with every individual person, should examine everything that presents real life, according to the archetype of beauty, design the life plan for the future in harmony with beauty, and guide life according to the idea of beauty" (Krause 2022: 247).

Virtue, law, divinity and beauty as the rational ends of human life to be realized at every level of each of the fundamental societies do not stand side by side unconnected in the Human League. But, as parts of the Human League, they stand in a reciprocal relation of mutual influence and fulfillment. For, in the end, they all arise from the one idea of humanity and may only be realized together:

> Each of the four fundamental forms (*Grundformen*) of all life demands to be formed as an independent idea purely according to its own law. And humankind devotes independent diligence to each of them, in a league dedicated to it exclusively. Nevertheless, these forms may be perfected at the same time, only in, with, and through each other, only in reciprocal association, and only in their consistent development (*Ausbildung*) is life in perfect form accomplished. These fundamental forms mutually presuppose each other, in the same essence, and exist already in predetermined harmony. (Krause 2022: 249)

Only if people, as part of a global civil society, have shaped the social world in such a way that a virtuous and beautiful life in legal security and religious freedom is not only formally but also materially possible for every human being, can there be the realization of the Human League on

Earth. For only then will Humankind have organized itself freely, according to the ideal of humanity and its dimensions of virtue, law, beauty, and divinity.[49]

4.2.3 The Laboring Societies for the Fundamental Works of Life

The purpose of the laboring societies for the fundamental works of life is that people gather in them to advance (a) science (*Wissenschaft*) and (b) art (*Kunst*) as necessary conditions for the development and perfection of the Human League.

(a) Science is a system of true findings, differentiated within itself, in which all parts "exist in relation to each other, not merely as a whole, in which parts are next to one other, collected in a mere aggregate, but as a whole in which all the parts are in, with and through one other [*in, mit und durch einander*], all only in, with and through, the whole" (Krause 1869: 4). Krause calls such a system of knowledge an "organism" and characterizes an organism as follows: "Everything is essentially joined to form a whole which contains parts, each of which, although something specific, and existing for itself, nevertheless exists only for itself, by, and as long, as it is in a certain connectedness, and interaction, with all other members of that structure [*Gliedern*], which also account for the organism" (Krause 1869: 4). Based on this concept of science, "the whole of knowledge is thought under the system of science, in which all particular items of knowledge are contained, as parts, related to each other and within the whole. Even the name 'science' [*Wissenschaft*] suggests this. And since parts, which are united in a whole, among themselves and with the whole, are called members [*Glieder*], science is thought as a related structure of its members [*Gliedbau*]" (Krause 1886a: 1). In the organic system of science, each individual item of scientific knowledge is logically and semantically connected, directly or indirectly, with some other item of knowledge. It is only by these logical and semantic compounds that any item is the item of knowledge it is. A single item of putative knowledge that stands alone, or that is not logically and semantically connected to the system as such, cannot exist in science according to Krause, because, through any single item of knowledge, all other true findings are, at least implicitly, given. The

---

49 For the current discussion, which Krause was already onto in 1811, cf. Benhabib (2016: 33): "For me, cosmopolitanism includes recognition that human beings are moral persons, equally entitled to legal protections, in virtue of rights accorded to them, not as nationals or members of an ethnic group, but as human beings themselves."

goal of science is knowledge of the Absolute and its intrinsic-relational determination, corresponding to the analytical-ascending and synthetic-descending part of philosophy.[50]

(b) Krause's concept of art as a counterpart to the concept of science includes not only the fine arts, but also achievements of arts useful in the technological sense. Science and art are thus the human ability to intervene creatively in the world within the framework of an ethic of responsibility, in order to realize the ideals of a dignified life: "Spirit (*Geist*), knowingly and with education, measures the natural law (*Naturgesetz*) of every being of organic and inorganic nature, yes, of the whole earth. Spirit intervenes, as a strange but friendly and gentle power, in the workshops of nature and awakens in her a second intimate but natural Creation. Spirit proclaims to Nature Spirit's power and dignity in the perfection and ennoblement of her own works. Spirit cultivates and educates with wisdom the plant world and the animal world and the human race. Spirit acts in the spirit of Nature itself, in agriculture and trades, as well as in the higher arts of chemistry, physics, physical education, and divine medicine" (Krause 2022: 56).[51]

As science and art advance, science and art enable an ever-closer approach to the realization of the Human League:

> In this way, with natural knowledge accomplished (*in vollkommner Naturerkenntnis*), Nature itself has passed into the consciousness of humankind. Then it can also be formed according to the eternal ideas which Reason is called upon by God to present in it (*in ihr darzustellen*). (Krause 1811a number 24: 95)

4.3 The Many Dimensions of Freedom

The driving historical force behind the historical establishment of the Human League, and the goal to be achieved through the Human League in higher perfection, is freedom for excellence. This kind of freedom for Krause is ethically, metaphysically and socially oriented, and consists of

---

50 Cf. Krause (2022: 48): "Because God, Nature, and Reason are the highest and singular (*einzigen*) ideas, the Science of God as *Ur-essence* is divided, according to its object, into: (a) the pure science of Reason, (b) independent pure natural science, and (c) the science of the consistent and changing life (*Wechselleben*) of Reason and Nature; between themselves (*unter sich*) and both for themselves (*für sich*) and united with God. As far as human nature allows, all people of all ages together must draw from all accessible sources of knowledge, in order to develop this Science uniformly in all its parts."

51 For the background to Krause's social theory, see Jonas (1979) and Latour (2001).

three dimensions: (1) freedom *from* external restrictions, (2) freedom *to* realize the humanity expressed in one's own individuality, and (3) freedom to associate *with* other people to realize this purpose.[52] For Krause, freedom thus is not exhausted by the quantity of possibilities of a free live, but consists in the qualitative possibilities of being able to lead an individual life in a dignified way, which presupposes not only formal human freedom but also the guarantee of material goods needed for a dignified life as a human being. In this, Krause's Human League proves to be a direct forerunner of the capability approach that is fiercely debated today.[53]

4.3.1 Freedom as the Driving Force of the Human League

Freedom is the driving force behind the historical realization of the Human League in all its dimensions because human beings, as free beings, cannot and must not be *forced* to realize the Human League. The development and founding of the cosmopolitan Human League as a global civil society can and must only take place through freedom. The realization of the ideal state of humanity is therefore not a philosophical-historical necessity, but only possible in and through the freedom of humanity as an expression of its historical creative power:

> Humanity is free, it can and should educate itself by free will (*in freiem Willen*). (Krause 1811a number 17: 68)

That is, all human beings are called to participate historically in the realization of the Human League:

> The human race must [...] grow little by little, spread over the whole earth, freely form all individual capacities and bring them to high excellence. The peoples must [...] form themselves independently. Then they will fight evil (*Uebel*) freely. (Krause 1900: 4)

In Krause's cosmopolitanism, therefore, any paternalism by social forces, or interventions by social institutions in social processes, are excluded from the promotion of the Human League, insofar as they are based on coercion. The establishment of the Human League may only be promoted through free dialogue.

---

52 Cf. Dierksmeier (2003: 572). See also Wollgast (1990: 100): "For K. Chr. F. Krause, freedom is therefore not empty independence or complete irresponsibility, but always freedom *for* something, not *from* something." For Krause, "human freedom" is therefore "fundamentally cosmopolitan and intergenerational" (Dierksmeier 2016a: 171). See also Ureña (2001: 451–452): "According to Rudolf Benfey, in Krause's *Human Archetype*, the new world principle of association is expressed for the first time in philosophy."

53 Cf. Conradi (1938: 30) and on today's debate, cf. Nussbaum (2016: 229).

For Krause, however, this does not rule out the possibility that some cultures are called upon to be teachers of other cultures:

> Mature peoples are called to educate underage, childlike, peoples. But, they have to educate themselves. And this education has to be: with love, with understanding, sensory (*sinniger*) and beautiful art, not selfish, but with the conscious intention of guiding all steps of development, to make the people's pupils (*Völker-Zöglinge*) mature, to make them equal, or even more beautiful and full of life than they are. (Krause 1900: 48)[54]

4.3.2 Freedom as the Goal of the Human League

Human freedom is not only the motive behind the establishment of the Human League. The complete freedom of humanity, and all human societies, is also the goal of the development of the Human League, because

> the Human League in its entire establishment (*Einrichtung*) and work function (*Werkthätigkeit*), [is] in pursuance of pure morality, and in particular of pure moral freedom (*reinsittlichen Freiheit*). (Krause 1820: lxxxxviii)

The individual freedom of humanity therefore is not only *ab ovo* a good, absolutely worth protecting, that global civil society "must keep sacred, promote, strengthen and preserve and make consistently inviolable" (Krause 1900: 2), but it can fully unfold itself and potentially realize its essence only in the Human League:

> As the highest society, the Human League does not disturb the freedom of any social institution. It allows everybody, as well as each single person, to develop freely. [...] In this way, the nascent Human League avoids the accusation of wishing to patronize humankind. For, it first wishes to come of age itself, and is never hasty, outwardly interfering, or disruptive. It works only internally, with the whole inner consistent power of the whole perfecting human being. (Krause 1900: 31)

That is:

> The Human League absolutely follows the principle of making the greatest possible freedom of every individual and every subordinate person [individual, BPG]

---

54 On the accusation of Eurocentrism for such a position, cf. Benhabib (2016: 189): "Today, popular sovereignty can no longer be restored by a return to the *black box* of state sovereignty: The formal equality of sovereign states must mean that human rights apply universally across state borders, and that rule of law and democratic forms of government are respected everywhere in the world. It is an insult to human dignity and the freedom of individuals to claim that human rights and cosmopolitan norms, as well as the condemnation of crimes against humanity, are solely products of a Western culture, the validity of which may not be extended to other peoples and cultures."

feasible and producible through social free will. And if not higher rights demand it, not to limit the freedom of the individual even in the smallest trifle. (Krause 1900: 255)

4.3.3 Cosmopolitanism and Cultural Diversity

Although the idea of the Human League is the free realization of a cosmopolitan civil society, and every human being should voluntarily participate in the realization of this ideal of humanity, the ideal state of human society does not involve the leveling of cultural differences. But rather, it emphasizes the cultural diversity of human life as the infinite formation of the one humanity, grounded in the Absolute:

> The peoples of the earth should and will retain their uniqueness. They will purify their uniquenes, exalt it, socialize it. They will be one humanity consisting of brother peoples. (Krause 1811a number 27: 116)

Because:

> Destroying the diversity of nations is neither possible nor desirable: This would mean dissolving the life of humanity itself. The purely humanely educated person (*der rein menschlich Gebildete*) gratefully acknowledges this institution of divine providence. They deeply revere and love the people of which they were born a member, to whom they owe most of their upbringing and the development of their personality. [...] But they are far from claiming more from their people than is due to them. They do not want all peoples to be like their own. They do not reject and despise anything because it is not like their home. (Krause 1811a: 37)[55]

That is, as Dierksmeier (2020a: 231) states:

> Krause in no way wishes to level the diversity of civilizations in that envisioned global federation of law, but rather especially aims to protect cultural diversity through the progress of cosmopolitan law. While, in a legally unregulated world, the economic and military powers of the day can raze traditional cultures as they please, weaker civilizations have much better chances for the preservation of their lifestyles in well-ordered bodies of cosmopolitan law. In other words, precisely because, for Krause, the earth belongs to all people and peoples for the realization

---

55 In the current debate, Held (2010: 76) also represents this point of view, which Krause had already presented in 1811: "It is important to stress that cosmopolitan philosophy does not deny the reality and ethical relevance of living in a world of diverse values and identities—how could it? It does not assume that unanimity is attainable on all practical-political questions." See also Pelluchon (2020: 337): "Cosmopolitanism does not blur the differences, and does not suppress the national level to which the citizens of a particular community relate. On the contrary, its importance consists in the recognition of the otherness of others, in the affirmation of the moral equality of people and cultures, and in the will to contribute to the solution of global problems."

of their individual freedom, the lifestyles of cultures may also manifest themselves in dissimilar ways.

The fact that cultural diversity is preserved in the Human League does not, however, imply an uncritical appropriation of past and superseded social structures: On the one hand, the historical contingency of previous human development must be included in the development of the Human League, and it must be noted that current social conditions are historically conditioned and therefore bring different starting points for the development of the Human League with them, because "each individual society [is] simultaneously dependent on the earlier and simultaneous state of all other *institutions* (*Institute*) existing alongside it, and ultimately on the state of human life as a whole" (Krause 1820: xxiv). On the other hand, it is precisely this historical awareness that enables a critical view of social conditions, which can show which structures can be adopted at all within the framework of a cosmopolitan civil society:

> Therefore I assert that what has been handed down, as such, and because it has been handed down, has no right, nor validity, to exist for all time, but only if, and to the extent that, it is still contemporary (*es noch jetzt zeitgemäß ist*). (Krause 1820: xxxviii)

Furthermore:

> *What was good for an earlier fulfilled life (Lebenvollzeit), what is essential for an earlier period of life (was einem frühern Lebenalter), becomes inappropriate for life as a result of development, as soon as the purpose of the earlier period is satisfied. Consequently it cannot and should not continue in life. And on the other hand: What was not yet required in the earlier period of life according to their idea and could not yet be achieved in it, That is now essential for the next period of life according to the new idea, required and has become possible to live. Therefore, in the future, with a new age and with a new full-time life, the new power comes into play to realize those ideas from now on, by which the intrinsic essence of this new life time is determined. If this thought is thought in its entirety, in its relation to the whole of life, then the very general and all-encompassing, general and universal, authority also results: to reshape and reshape the whole of life steadily, artistically, according to the progress of the development of the organism of ideas in time.* (Krause 1843: 277–278)

Those social structures that hinder the free development of the Human League must be overcome, historically and socially, through politics; as an expression of the social will, directed toward the realization of the Human League.[56]

---

56 Cf. also Krause (1811a: 4): Science "should recognize and love the good and beautiful, of the past and the present. It teaches how what is traditionally good

4.4 Utopia of the Not-Yet

If freedom is both the starting point and the goal of the development of the Human League, then it follows that the more fully the Human League is established as the social framework for the realization of this freedom, the more perfectly human freedom will be realized, because "humankind lives in its individuals" (Krause 1811a: 6). Freedom is, in other words, subject to the law of accelerating returns: The freedom of the individual and the realization of the Human League as an ideal of social freedom are in a reciprocal organic relationship and mutually dependent.[57] It was therefore clear to Krause that "everything human [only] appears in its true light in the idea of humanity as a whole" (Krause 1811a: 2) because "it is the idea of humanity in which every individual, every people, every family, and every society, must design their ideal" (Krause 1900: 14). However, although the individual is always already influenced in their thinking, feeling, and will, by the (historical) society in which they stand, and have been socialized[58], the individual is in principle in a position to change social conditions according to the ideal of humanity through their own free action, and thus to become more perfect as an individual within society:

> [T]he individual human being and human society stand in essential union and indissoluble interaction. The individual receives a large part of their intellectual formation from society. Their whole mental life is determined, maintained, sustained, promoted, and hindered, by their social circumstances. Conversely, however, the individual human being, as an individual soul, has in turn a powerful and intimate effect on the soul life (*Seelenleben*) of entire societies. Yes: If the individual succeeds in bringing a fundamental idea (*grundwesenliche Idee*) into their individual consciousness and teaches this with clarity to humankind, it can happen that the single individual spirit determines the spirit of all humankind, and stimulates it to higher life. (Krause 1848: 7)

The Human League is the all-encompassing human civil society in which the ideal of humanity is socially realized out of and in freedom. It enables every individual, and every social league, to freely realize their essence. The realization of this cosmopolitan society lies in the hands of Humanity

---

and beautiful in itself may be freely and artistically redesigned and educated according to the spirit of the present for the near future."
57 See also Ter Meulen (1929: 110): "As Krause teaches us in his *Urbild der Menschheit*, the history of humankind is the development of its organization."
58 Cf. Krause (1811a (9): 9): "Having emerged alone from human society, and simply living in it, the individual finds itself bound to it on all sides." Cf. also Krause (1820: iv): "Just as everything human only thrives in society, the higher *Zeitgeist* will awaken a new bond for this newly forming part of human life as well."

itself. Therefore, the ideal of the Human League as an expression of freedom is not only a postulate of Practical Reason but also a utopia of the *not-yet*, with the purpose of changing social reality, and the self-perception of humanity. As Krause puts it: "The aim of life is an attainable one, set before [Humankind] by God for eternity, not an unattainable goal in the mist of the infinite distance" (Krause 1843: 116).[59]

Krause was sure that the idea of the Human League, as the idea of an ideal global civil society for the realization of true humanity, is appealing to every human being:

> This doctrine of the essential life of humankind and of the Human League is so simple, so spiritual and pleasant (*angemüthig*) (appealing to the heart) (*anherzig*), so easy to understand, and speaks to every still uncorrupted heart so easily and so intimately that only a few generations will pass until the time when the comrades of the more educated people (*Genossen der gebildeteren Völker*) could hardly imagine how a time was possible in which people did not have this insight and this feeling (*diese Einsicht und dieses Gefühl*)." (Krause 1890: 123)[60]

Therefore, there was no doubt for Krause that the Human League as a global civil society can and will be historically realized through the free cooperation of people.

---

59 What Höffe (2016: 262) says about Kant's world republic also applies to Krause's Human League: "The world republic is not an enthusiastic utopia of fundamentally nowhere (*schwärmerische Utopie des grundsätzlichen Nirgendwo*). Rational law (*Rechtsvernunft*) does not give itself up to dreams that distort reality, to personal or collective illusions. What it demands, a World-State with a democratic constitution, a secondary state world republic, is something else: a utopia of the *not-yet*, a political ideal that we are already on the way to realizing." See also Dierksmeier (2003: 572): "From 1803, Christian Friedrich Krause worked out a *Philosophy of Freedom* that [...] was principally based on social 'harmony'. In Krause's liberalism, the good and just actions (*Handeln*) of people in the areas of politics, law, economy, education, religion etc. are given special consideration. Krause wishes to build a social framework in which individuals may realize their striving for the good, based on the basic values of freedom, equality, and independence." See also Habermas (2016: 379): "The cosmopolitan expansion of the initially established domestic legal situation is not only desirable for the sake of eternal peace, but as such is a requirement of Practical Reason."

60 See Krause (1820: xi). See also Schneider (1907: 361).

Conclusion

Krause develops his cosmopolitanism against the background of his panentheistic metaphysics. In Krause's panentheistic cosmopolitanism, the structure of the Human League as a global civil society is the structure of a functionally differentiated society: In the Human League, ultimately, every individual, every family, every friendship, every nation, every league of peoples, and finally, the global civil society itself realize the ideals of virtue, law, beauty, and divinity that suits them in order to realize the ideal of humanity. Because in Krause's system of philosophy, humanity is at the center of the Absolute, as the union of Reason and Nature, humanity is called upon, and is capable of realizing, the league of humanity as the temporal image of the Absolute, in and by freedom for excellence. Against this background of Krause's panentheistic cosmopolitanism, Benz (1955: 87) is therefore right in stating that

> the UN could rightly appoint [Krause] as its court philosopher (*Hofphilosophen*), because it was Krause who developed the idea in numerous writings, above all in his *The Human Archetype*, that humankind will develop beyond the level of nation-state organization […] into a World-State. This, after shedding state shackles, will be changed into the form of a free Human League.[61]

The Human League as a society of societies is the realization of the ideal of humanity, which is based on the idea of the absolute equal value of all human beings, in particular of all men and women. As Wollgast (1990: 87) states: "There is certainly no other representative of classical German philosophy who treated the idea of female equality as decisively as Krause." Within this framework of a cosmopolitan civil society, the Human League provides every human being with the formal and material conditions for a dignified life in and by moral freedom:

> As fantastic as this outline appeared when it was implemented in 1811, the underlying idea of voluntary co-operation between social units is basically also the concept of institutionalized conflict resolution mechanisms in modern pluralistic societies. (Groß 2008: 25)

As a philosophy of freedom, all of this is not only readily consistent with the current debates on the justification of human rights but is also to be understood as a historically early formulation of the neo-Aristotelian capability approach. Furthermore, in view of the ecological crisis of our time,

---

61 Cf. also Cavallar (2003: 183): "Krause was not primarily a mastermind of the European Union, but one of the intellectual fathers of the United Nations."

Krause's panentheism may also be connected to debates about the rights of Nature in general, and the rights of animals in particular. For, for Krause, Nature is a determination of the Absolute that is absolutely equivalent to the Spirit, and therefore has intrinsic value. As Groß (2008: 135–136) argues:

> Preserving Nature without damaging it, already anticipates modern ecological ideas. Krause derives his duty to Nature from analytical natural philosophy on the one hand, and from speculative theology on the other. Analytically, the human being recognizes that Nature does not confront them as contrary, but that they already represents it with their body (*Leib*). Synthetically, the human being has the certainty that Nature is not an alien force (*eine fremde Macht*), but that, like Reason, it is a power of Ur-Essence (*eine Potenz Urwesens*). The duty towards Nature is an existential concern of the human being, who does not want to destroy their natural environment (*Lebenswelt*).

Brüninghaus (1993: 30) comes to a similar conclusion:

> Karl Christian Friedrich Krause (1781–1832) deserves credit for being the first philosopher to have designed a real system of animal ethics. [...] So, the human being has a moral obligation towards the animal, because love commands the human to recognize the dignity of the other, and animals also belong to these "others."

In conclusion, one may therefore agree with Ureña/Fuchs (2007: vii–viii): "that there is no doubt that Krause deserves a place of honor in post-Kantian German idealism alongside Fichte, Schelling and Hegel." This is because "Krause is indispensable alongside Fichte, Schelling and Hegel, at the core of German idealism" (Ureña and Fuchs 2007: ix–x).

Bibliography

Ahrens, Heinrich. 1871. *Naturrecht oder die Philosophie des Rechts und des Staates auf dem Grunde des Zusammenhanges von Recht und Cultur.* Band 2. Vienna.

Albrecht, Andrea. 2005. *Kosmopolitismus. Weltbürgerdiskurse in Literatur, Philosophie und Publizistik um 1800.* Berlin: Walter de Gruyter.

App, Urs. 2014. *Schopenhauer's Compass.* Wil, Switzerland: University Media.

Benhabib, Seyla. 2004. *The Rights of Others. Aliens, Residents and Citizens.* Cambridge.

Benhabib, Seyla. 2016. *Kosmopolitismus ohne Illusionen. Menschenrechte in unruhigen Zeiten.* Berlin: Suhrkamp.

Benz, Ernst. 1955. *Schelling. Werden und Wirken seines Denkens.* Zürich.

Brüninghaus, Birgit. 1993. *Die Stellung des Tieres im Bürgerlichen Gesetzbuch.* Berlin: Duncker & Humblot.

Cavallar, Georg. 2003. 'Abschied von der internationalen Anarchie: Die einer europäischen Union bei Krause und Schmidt-Phiseldek' In: *Wiener Jahrbuch für Philosophie.* Vol. XXXV. 169–190.

Conradi, Franz Ferdinand. 1938. *Karl Christian Friedrich Krauses Rechtsphilosophie in ihren Grundideen.* Strasbourg: Heitz & Co.

Dierksmeier, Claus. 1999. "Karl Christian Friedrich Kause und das 'gute Recht.'" In: *Archiv für Rechts- und Sozialphilosophie.* Vol. 85 (1). 75–94.

Dierksmeier, Claus. 2003. "Die Wirschaftsphilosophie des 'Krausismo.'" In: *Deutsche Zeitschrift für Philosophie.* Vol. 51 (4). 571–581.

Dierksmeier, Claus. 2003a. *Der Absolute Grund des Rechts. Karl Christian Friedrich Krause in Auseinandersetzung mit Fichte und Schelling.* Stuttgart-Bad Cannstatt.

Dierksmeier, Claus. 2008. "From Karl Christian Friedrich Krause (1781–1832) to 'Krausismo.'" In: *APA Newsletter.* Vol. 8 (1). 14–22.

Dierksmeier, Claus. 2013. "Krausism." In: Susana Nuccetelli, Ofelia Schutte, Otávio Bueno (Hrsg.): *A Companion to Latin American Philosophy.* Oxford: Wiley-Blackwell. 110–127.

Dierksmeier, Claus. 2016. "Umwelt als Mitwelt. Die päpstliche Enzyklika *Laudato si´* und der argentinische *Krausismo*" In: *Kirche und Gesellschaft.* Vol. 428. 3–16.

Dierksmeier, Claus. 2016a. *Qualitative Freiheit. Selbstbestimmung in weltbürgerlicher Verantwortung.* Bielefeld: transcript.

Dierksmeier, Claus. 2020a. "Global Citizenship and Cosmopolitan Governance in the Legal Philosophy of K.C.F. Krause." In: *Rechtsphilosophie*. Vol. 6 (3). 221–233.

Gil, Thomas. 1988. "Immanuel Kant, K.C.F. Krause und J. Sanz Del Río. Praktisches Interesse und Versittlichung in der Geschichts- und Gesellschaftstheorie." In: Jorge Eugenio Dotti, Harald Holz, Hans Radermacher (Hrsg.): *Kant in der Hispanidad*. Bern, New York: Peter Lang. 97–110.

Glasenapp, Helmuth von. 1956. "Indien in der Gedankenwelt des Philosophen Karl Christian Friedrich Krause." In: H. O. Günther (Hrsg.): *Indien und Deutschland. Ein Sammelband*. Europäische Verlagsanstalt. 16–22.

Gott, Richard. 2002. "Karl Krause and the Ideological Origins of the Cuban Revolution." In: *University of London. Institute of Latin American Studies*. Occasional Papers. Vol. 28. 1–16.

Göcke, Benedikt Paul. 2012. *Alles in Gott? Zur Aktualität des Panentheismus Karl Christian Friedrich Krauses*. Friedrich Pustet.

Göcke, Benedikt Paul. 2018. *The Panentheism of Karl Christian Friedrich Krause (1781–1832). From Transcendental Philosophy to Metaphysics*. Oxford, Berlin: Peter Lang.

Göcke, Benedikt Paul. 2020. "Karl Christian Friedrich Krause's Influence on Schopenhauer's Philosophy." In: Robert Wicks (Hrsg.): *The Oxford Handbook of Schopenhauer*. Oxford: Oxford University Press. 2020. 29–48.

Göcke, Benedikt Paul. 2021. "Karl Christian Friedrich Krauses Einfluss auf Arthur Schopenhauers 'Die Welt als Wille und Vorstellung.'" In: *Archiv für Geschichte der Philosophie*. Vol. 103 (1). 148–168.

Göcke, Benedikt Paul. 2022. "Das Urbild der Menschheit. Panentheismus als kosmopolitische Gesellschaftstheorie." In: Benedikt Paul Göcke, Johannes Seidel SJ (Hrsg.): *Karl Christian Friedrich Krause: Das Urbild der Menschheit*. Philosophische Bibliothek. Hamburg: Meiner-Verlag. ix–cvii.

Göcke, Benedikt Paul. 2022a. "Panentheism as Cosmopolitanism: Karl Christian Friedrich Krause's Conception of a Global Human Leage." In: *Religious Studies*. Online First.

Groß, Stefan. 2008. *Die Metaphysik Karl Christian Friedrich Krauses in ihrem Verhältnis zu Religio, Ethik und Ästhetik*. Frankfurt am Main: Peter Lang.

Habermas, Jürgen. 2016. "Hat die Konstitutionalisierung des Völkerrechts noch eine Chance? Politisch verfasste Weltgesellschaft vs. Weltrepublik (Auszug)." In: Christoph Broszies, Henning Hahn (Hrsg.): *Globale Gerechtigkeit. Schlüsseltexte zur Debatte zwischen Partikularismus und Kosmopolitismus*. Berlin: Suhrkamp. 373–403.

Held, David. 2010. *Cosmopolitanism. Ideals and Realities.* Cambridge: Polity Press.

Hofmann, Hasso. 1988. "Natur und Naturschutz im Spiegel des Verfassungsrechts." In: *Juristen Zeitung.* Vol. 43. 265–316.

Hohlfeld, Paul. 1879. *Die Krause'sche Philosophie in ihrem geschichtlichen Zusammenhange und in ihrer Bedeutung für das Geistesleben der Gegenwart.* Jena: Hermann Costenoble.

Hohlfeld, Paul. 1892. "Johann Amos Comenius und Karl Christian Friedrich Krause." In: *Monatshefte der Comenius-Gesellschaft.* Vol. 1. 1–15.

Hohlfeld, Paul, August Wünsche. 1903. *Der Briefwechsel Karl Christian Friedrich Krauses zur Würdigung seines Lebens und Wirkens.* Aus dem Handschriftlichen Nachlasse herausgegeben. Band 1. Leipzig: Dieterichsche Verlangsbuchhandlung.

Hohlfeld, Paul, August Wünsche. 1907. *Der Briefwechsel Karl Christian Friedrich Krauses zur Würdigung seines Lebens und Wirkens.* Aus dem Handschriftlichen Nachlasse herausgegeben. Band 2. Leipzig: Dieterichsche Verlangsbuchhandlung.

Horn, Reinhard. 1985. "Der Einfluß freimaurerischer Ideen auf Krauses 'Urbild der Menschheit.'" In: Klaus-M. Kodalle (Hrsg.): *Der Vernunftfrieden. Kants Entwurf im Widerstreit.* Würzburg: Königshausen & Neumann. 124–132.

Höffe, Otfried. 2016. "Für und wider eine Weltrepublik." In: Christoph Broszies, Henning Hahn (Hrsg.): *Globale Gerechtigkeit. Schlüsseltexte zur Debatte zwischen Partikularismus und Kosmopolitismus.* Berlin: Suhrkamp. 242–262.

Jiménez García, A. 1994. *El Krausismo y la Institution Libre de Enseñanza.* Madrid: ediciones pedagógicas.

Jonas, Hans. 1979. *Das Prinzip Verantwortung.* Frankfurt am Main: Suhrkamp.

Krause, Karl Christian Friedrich. 1804. *Entwurf des Systems der Philosophie. Erste Abtheilung enthaltend die allgemeine Philosophie, nebst einer Anleitung zur Naturphilosophie. Für seine Vorlesungen.* Jena und Leipzig.

Krause, Karl Christian Friedrich. 1811a. *Tagblatt des Menschheitlebens.* Erster Jahrgang. Erstes Vierteljahr für die Monate Januar, Februar, März, nebst einem literarischen Anzeiger. Dresden: Arnoldinische Buchhandlung.

Krause, Karl Christian Friedrich. 1820. *Die die ältesten Kunsturkunden der Freimaurerbrüderschaft, mitgetheilt, bearbeitet und in einem Lehrfragstükke urvergeistiget.* Zweite, neubearbeite, mit dem Lehrlingsrituale des neuenglischen Zweiges de Bruderschaft, sowie mit einigen anderen Kunsturkunden und Abhandlungen vermehrte Ausgabe. Erster Band. In zwei Abtheilungen. Dresden: Arnoldinische Buchhandlung.

Krause, Karl Christian Friedrich. 1820a. *Höhere Vergeistigung der echt überlieferten Grundsymbole der Freimaurerei in zwölf Logenvorträgen. Dritte, unveränderte, mit einer Uebersicht des Zwekkes und Inhaltes der Schrift desselben Verfassers:* über die drei ältesten Kunsturkunden der Freimaurerbrüderschaft, *vermehrte Ausgabe.* Dresden.

Krause, Karl Christian Friedrich. 1828. *Vorlesungen über das System der Philosophie.* Göttingen: Dieterische Buchhandlung.

Krause, Karl Christian Friedrich. 1829. *Vorlesungen über die Grundwahrheiten der Wissenschaft, zugleich in ihrer Beziehung zuzugleich in ihrer Beziehung zu dem Leben. Nebst einer kurzen Darstellung* und Würdigung der bisherigen Systeme der Philosophie, vornehmlich der neusten von Kant, Fichte, Schelling und Hegel, und der Lehre Jacobi's. Göttingen: Dieterische Buchhandlung.

Krause, Karl Christian Friedrich. 1836. *Die Lehre vom Erkennen und von der Erkenntniss, als erste Einleitung in die Wissenschaft. Vorlesungen für Gebildete aus allen Ständen.* Herausgegeben von Germann Karl von Leonhardi. Göttingen: Dieterich'sche Verlagsbuchhandlung.

Krause, Karl Christian Friedrich. 1843. *Die reine d.i. allgemeine Lebenlehre und Philosophie der Geschichte zu Begründung der Lebenkunstwissenschaft. Vorlesungen für Gebildete aus allen Ständen.* In einem Bande, herausgegeben von Hermann Karl von Leonhardi. Göttingen: In Commission der Dieterich'schen Buchhandlung.

Krause, Karl Christian Friedrich. 1848. *Vorlesungen über die psychische Anthropologie.* Herausgegeben von Dr. H. Ahrens. Göttingen: In Commission der Dieterich'schen Buchhandlung.

Krause, Karl Christian Friedrich. 1868. *Erneute Vernunftkritik.* Prag: Verlag von F. Tempsky.

Krause, Karl Christian Friedrich. 1869. *Der zur Gewissheit der Gotteserkenntnis als des höchsten Wissenschaftsprinzips emporleitende Theil der Philosophie,* Prag: F. Tempsky.

Krause, Karl Christian Friedrich. 1873. *Der Glaube an die Menschheit, die Gebote der Menschlichkeit und die Vergeistigung des Vaterunsers.* Prag: F. Tempsky.

Krause, Karl Christian Friedrich. 1874. *Das System der Rechtsphilosophie. Vorlesungen für Gebildete aus allen Ständen*, herausgegeben von Karl David August Röder. Leipzig: F.A. Brockhaus.

Krause, Karl Christian Friedrich. 1886. *Abriss des Systems der Philosophie.* Leipzig: Otto Schulze.

Krause, Karl Christian Friedrich. 1889. *Philosophische Abhandlungen.* Aus dem handschriftlichen Nachlasse des Verfassers, herausgegeben von Paul Hohlfeld und August Wünsche, Leipzig: Otto Schulze.

Krause, Karl Christian Friedrich. 1890. *Das Eigenthümliche der Wesenlehre nebst Nachrichten zur Geschichte der Aufnahme derselben, vornehmlich von Seiten deutscher Philosophen*. Aus dem handschriftlichen Nachlasse des Verfassers herausgegeben von Dr. Paul Hohlfeld und Dr. August Wünsche. Leipzig: Otto Schulze.

Krause, Karl Christian Friedrich. 1890a. *Anschauungen oder Lehren und Entwürfe zur Höherbildung des Menschheitlebens*. Aus dem Handschriftllichen Nachlasse des Verfassers herausgegeben von Dr. Paul Hohlfeld und Dr. August Wünsche. Band 1. Leipzig: Otto Schulze.

Krause, Karl Christian Friedrich. 1891. *Anschauungen oder Lehren und Entwürfe zur Höherbildung des Menschheitlebens*. Aus dem Handschriftllichen Nachlasse des Verfassers herausgegeben von Dr. Paul Hohlfeld und Dr. August Wünsche. Band 2. Leipzig: Otto Schulze.

Krause, Karl Christian Friedrich. 1892. *Anschauungen oder Lehren und Entwürfe zur Höherbildung des Menschheitlebens*. Aus dem Handschriftllichen Nachlasse des Verfassers herausgegeben von Dr. Paul Hohlfeld und Dr. August Wünsche. Band 3. Leipzig: Otto Schulze.

Krause, Karl Christian Friedrich. 1892a. *Anfangsgründe der Erkenntnislehre, aus dem handschriftlichen Nachlasse des Verfassers,* herausgegeben von Paul Hohlfeld und August Wünsche, Leipzig: Otto Schulze.

Krause, Karl Christian Friedrich. 1892b. *Zur Religionsphilosophie und speculativen Theologie*, aus dem handschriftlichen Nachlasse des Verfassers herausgegeben von Paul Hohlfeld und August Wünsche, Leipzig: Otto Schulze.

Krause, Karl Christian Friedrich. 1892d. Vorlesungen über Naturrecht oder Philosophie des Rechts und des Staates. Hg. von R. Mucke.

Krause, Karl Christian Friedrich. 1893a. *Der Begriff der Philosophie*, aus dem handschriftlichen Nachlasse, herausgegeben von Paul Hohlfeld und August Wünsche, Leipzig: Otto Schulze.

Krause, Karl Christian Friedrich. 1893. *Der Erdrechtsbund an sich selbst und in seinem Verhältnisse zum Ganzen und zu allen Einzeltheilen des Menschheitlebens*. Aus dem handschriftlichen Nachlasse des Verfassers herausgegeben von Dr. Georg Mollat. Leipzig Otto Schulze.

Krause, Karl Christian Friedrich. 1889. *Zur Geschichte der neueren philosophischen Systeme*, aus dem handschriftlichen Nachlasse des Verfassers, herausgegeben von Paul Hohlfeld und August Wünsche, Leipzig: Otto Schulze.

Krause, Karl Christian Friedrich. 1900. *Der Menschheitbund nebst Anhang und Nachträgen*. Aus dem Handschriftliche Nachlasse von Karl Chr. Fr. Krause herausgegeben von Richard Vetter. Berlin: Verlag von Emil Felber.

Krause, Karl Christian Friedrich. 1905. *Vorlesungen über psychische Anthropologie*. Herausgegeben von Paul Hohlfeld und August Wünsche. Leipzig: Dieterich'sche Verlagsbuchhandlung.

Krause, Karl Christian Friedrich. 2007. *Entwurf des Systemes der Philosophie. Erste Abteilung, enthaltend die allgemeine Philosophie, nebst einer Anleitung zur Naturphilosophie*, Stuttgart: Frommann-Holzboog, edited by Enrique Ureña und Eruch Fuchs.

Krause, Karl Christian Friedrich. 2022. *Das Urbild der Menschheit*, edited by Benedikt Göcke and Johannes Seidel SJ. Hamburg: Felix Meiner.

Kreiser, Lothar. 2001. *Gottlob Frege. Leben—Werk—Zeit*. Hamburg: Felix Meiner.

Krumpel, Heinz. 1990. "Karl Christian Friedrich Krause und der Krausismo—Ein Beispiel außergewöhnlicher Wirkung deutscher Philosophie in Spanien und Lateinamerika." In: *Wiener Jahrbuch für Philosophie*. Vol. XXII. 155–168.

Krumpel, Heinz. 2001. "Zur Aneignung und Verwandlung der Ideen Humboldts und Krauses in Lateinamerika. Gemeinsamkeiten und Unterschiede." In: *International Review for Humboldtian Studies*. Vol. II (2). 1–10.

Landau, Peter. 1995. *Stufen der Gerechtigkeit. Zur Rechtsphilosophie von Gottfried Wilhelm Leibniz und Karl Christian Friedrich Krause*. Munich: Verlag der Bayerischen Akademie der Wissenschaften.

Latour, Buno. 2001. *Das Parlament der Dinge. Für eine politische Ökologie*. Frankfurt am Main.

Leonhardi, Hermann. 1905. *Karl Christian Friedrich Krause als philosophischer Denker gewürdigt*. Aus dem philosophischen Nachlasse des Verfassers herausgegeben von Dr. Paul Hohlfeld und Dr. August Wünsche. Leipzig: Dieterich'sche Verlagsbuchhhandlung.

López-Morillas, Juan. 1981. *The Krausist Movement and ideological change in Spain, 1864–1874*. Cambridge: Cambridge University Press.

Mateo, Rogelio García. 1982. *Das deutsche Denken und das moderne Spanien. Panentheismus als Wissenschaftssystem bei Karl Chr. Fr. Krause. Seine Interpretation und Wirkungsgeschichte in Spanien: Der Spanische Krausismus*. Frankfurt am Main, Bern: Peter Lang.

Medhananda, Swami. 2022. Panentheism and the "Most Nonsensical Superstition" of Polytheism: A Critical Examination of K.C.F. Krause's Reception of Vedānta and Hindu Religion' In: *European Journal for Philosophy of Religion*.

Meixner, Uwe. 2022. "K. C. F. Krause: The Combinatorian as Logician." In: *European Journal for Philosophy of Religion*.

Nussbaum, Martha C. 2016. "Jenseits des Gesellschaftsvertrags. Fähigkeiten und globale Gerechtigkeit." In: Christoph Broszies, Henning Hahn (Hrsg.): *Globale Gerechtigkeit. Schlüsseltexte zur Debatte zwischen Partikularismus und Kosmopolitismus.* Berlin: Suhrkamp. 209–241.

Pelluchon, Corine. 2020. *Wovon wir leben. Eine Philosophie der Ernährung und der Umwelt.* Darmstadt: wbg.

Proksch, Alfred. 1880. *Karl Christian Friedrich Krause. Ein Lebensbild nach seinen Briefen dargestellt.* Leipzig: Grunow.

Rabe, Christine Susanne. 2006. "Die Stellung der Frau bei Karl Christian Friedrich Krause und seinen Schülern." In: Stephan Meder, Arne Duncker, Andrea Czelk (Hrsg.): *Frauenrecht und Rechtsgeschichte. Die Rechtskämpfe der deutschen Frauenbewegung.* Köln: Böhlau Verlag. 89–98.

Rabe, Christine Susanne. 2006a. *Gleichwertigkeit von Mann und Frau. Die Krause-Schule und die bürgerliche Frauenbewegung im 19. Jahrhundert.* Köln: Böhlau.

Rathore, Aakash Singh, Rimina Mohapatra. 2018. *Hegel's India. A Reinterpretation with Texts.* New Delhi: Oxford University Press.

Reinhardt, Karoline. 2021. *Migration und Weltbürgerrecht. Zur Aktualität eines Theoriestücks der politischen Philosophie Kants.* Munich: Karl Alber.

Riedel, Kurt. 1954. *Fast vollständige Karl Chr. Fr. Krause—Bücherkunde und ausführliche Krause-Nachlaß-Bibliographie, Erste Abteilung: Nachlaß-Bibliographie, 7. Lieferung: Briefe von, an und über Karl Chr. Fr. Krause* (unpublished typed manuscript held in University of Dresden Library).

Rödl, Florian. 2017. "Zur Kritik rechtspositivistischer Menschenrechtskonzeption." In: Margit Wasmaier-Sailer, Matthias Hoesch (Hrsg.): *Die Begründung der Menschenrechte. Kontroversen im Spannungsfeld von positivem Recht, Naturrecht und Vernunftrecht.* Tübingen: Mohr Siebeck. 29–42.

Rubio, Christian. 2017. *Krausism and the Spanish Avant-Garde. The Impact of Philosophy on National Culture.* New York: Cambria Press.

Schmitz, Sabine. 2000. *Spanischer Naturalismus. Entwurf eines epochēnprofils im Kontext des "Krausopositivismo."* Tübingen: Max Niemeyer.

Schneider, Theodor. 1907. *Karl Christian Friedrich Krause als Geschichtsphilosoph.* Leipzig: Bär & Hermann.

Ter Meulen, Jacob. 1929. *Der Gedanke der Internationalen Organisation in seiner Entwicklung.* Zweiter Band: 1789–1889. Erstes Stück: 1789–1870. The Hague: Martinus Nijhoff.

Ureña, E. M. 1988. "El fraude de Sanz del Río o la verdad sobre su Ideal de la Humanidad." In: *Pensamiento. Revista de investigación e información filosófica.* Vol. 44. 25–47.

Ureña, E. M. 1991. *K. C. F. Krause. Philosoph, Freimaurer, Weltbürger, Eine Biographie*. Stuttgart-Bad Cannstatt: frommann-holzboog.

Ureña, E. M. 2001. *Philosophie und gesellschaftliche Praxis. Wirkungen der Philosophie K. C. F. Krauses in Deutschland*. Stuttgart-Bad Cannstatt: frommann-holzboog.

Ureña, E. M. 2007. *Die Krause-Rezeption in Deutschland im 19. Jahrhundert. Philosophie—Religion—Staat*. Stuttgart-Bad Cannstatt: frommann-holzboog.

Ureña, Enrique M., Erich Fuchs. 2007. "Einführung in das Gesamtwerk." In: Krause 2007.

Ureña, Enrique M, Pedro Álvarez Lázaro, Ricardo Pinilla Burgos, José Manel Vázquez-Romero, Andrea Schäpers (Hrsg.). 2018. *Karl Christian Friedrich Krause. Band V. Das Urbild der Menschhiet. Ein Versuch. Dresden 1811*. Stuttgart-Bad Cannstatt.

Vester, Wolfgang. 1933. *Sozialphilosophie und Sozialpolitik der deutschen Rechtsphilosophie des XIX. Jahrhunderts. (Krause, Ahrens, Röder)*. Dissertation zur Erlangung der Doktorwürde bei der Philosophischen Fakultät der Hessischen Ludwigs-Universität zu Gießen. Cottbus: Gebr. Grosse.

Wirmer-Donos, Bettina. 2001. *Die Strafrechtstheorie Karl Christian Friedrich Krauses als theoretische Grundlage des spanischen Korrektionalismus*. Frankfurt am Main: Peter Lang.

Wollgast, Siegfried. 1990. *Karl Christian Friedrich Krause (1781–1832)—ein deutscher Philosoph mit Weltgeltung*. Sitzungsberichte der Sächsischen Akademie der Wissenschaften zu Leipzig. Philologisch-Historische Klasse Band 129 (5). Berlin: Akademie Verlag. 65–108.

Wollgast, Siegfried. 2016. *Karl Christian Friedrich Krause. Aspekte von Leben, Werk, Wirkung*. Berlin: Weidler Buchverlag.

www.ingramcontent.com/pod-product-compliance
Ingram Content Group UK Ltd.
Pitfield, Milton Keynes, MK11 3LW, UK
UKHW041913140426
5217IPUK00002B/30